Walking in
Your Own
Shoes

Walking in Your Own Shoes

DISCOVER GOD'S DIRECTION
FOR YOUR LIFE

ROBERT A. SCHULLER

with William Kruidenier

Foreword by Dr. Phil McGraw

New York   Boston   Nashville

Unless otherwise indicated, Scriptures are taken from the HOLY BIBLE: NEW INTERNATIONAL VERSION®. Copyright © 1973, 1978, 1984 by International Bible Society. Used by permission of Zondervan Publishing House. All rights reserved.

Scriptures noted The Message are taken from The Message. Copyright © 1993, 1994, 1995, 1996, 2000, 2001, 2002. Used by permission of NavPress Publishing Group.

Scriptures noted NLT are taken from the *Holy Bible*, New Living Translation, copyright © 1996. Used by permission of Tyndale House Publishers, Inc., Wheaton, Illinois 60189. All rights reserved.

Scriptures noted NKJV are taken from the NEW KING JAMES VERSION. Copyright © 1979, 1980, 1982, Thomas Nelson, Inc., Publishers.

Scriptures noted NASB are taken from the New American Standard Bible®, Copyright © 1960, 1962, 1963, 1968, 1972, 1975, 1977, 1995 by The Lockman Foundation. Used by permission.

FaithWords
Hachette Book Group
237 Park Avenue
New York, NY 10017

Visit our Web site at www.faithwords.com.

Printed in the United States of America

Originally published in hardcover by Hachette Book Group.

First Trade Edition: January 2009
10 9 8 7 6 5 4 3 2 1

FaithWords is a division of Hachette Book Group, Inc.
The FaithWords name and logo are trademarks of Hachette Book Group, Inc.

The Library of Congress has cataloged the hardcover edition as follows:
    Schuller, Robert A.
        Walking in your own shoes : discover God's direction for your life / Robert A. Schuller. — 1st ed.
            p.   cm.
        ISBN-13: 978-0-446-58097-7
        ISBN-10: 0-446-58097-X
        1. Vocation—Christianity. 2. Christian life. I. Title.
        BV4740.S325 2007
        248.4 — dc22   2007018768

ISBN 978-0-446-69977-8 (pbk.)

DEDICATION

Anthony was a farmer who was born in the nineteenth century. It was a time when only the privileged went to college and grad school. Thus, the hopes of many talented people went unfulfilled. It was a cast system that was difficult to bridge and only a few were successful. Anthony was not successful. He did not manage to break out and fulfill his dream for his life. He had always wanted to be a Dominee.

The Dominee was the most respected man in his community. He directed the Dutch settlers spiritually and socially. He gathered everyone on a regular basis for teaching, admonition, and special occasions. He was there whenever there was a death. No one was married without his blessing. Socials were always held next to his home. If there was a tragedy, he was there to comfort the family. The Dominee was the glue of the community. He was the judge and jury. He was the highest judicial in the surroundings. He was their minister; their pastor.

But Anthony was never able to afford the schooling necessary to rise to that position. He never went past the eighth grade. He had to help his family survive. It was tough in his day. If your crops failed you starved. They were extremely poor. The farm provided the only means of survival and manual labor was the key to success on the farm. It was long, backbreaking work. The entire family pitched in. If you wanted to eat you had a role and responsibility. The youngest helped with the chickens. As they grew, they moved to the pigs and then the cows. All of the chores were shared. It was the backbone of the "Greatest" generation that founded the fabric of the United States of America in the twentieth century. Anthony gave his dream to his bothers, sisters, and parents so the farm could continue and the family could have the dignity of sitting in church, paying their tithes, and knowing that through their labor and God's providence, they were there together.

As time moved on, Anthony's dream shifted to his children. He decided that if he couldn't be a Dominee, then maybe he could have a son who would be. Women's rights weren't where they are today and only a male could rise to that position so he prayed for a son and God answered his prayer. He named him Henry after his brother in law who was a Dominee and missionary. The highest calling a Dominee could have was to be a missionary. Henry was the crown jewel of the family and a fitting name for Anthony's first son who would be the next Dominee.

But Henry had no interest in Anthony's dream. Henry loved the farm. He enjoyed the solitude, the labor, the satisfaction of watching God's hand at work in the birth of a calf, and seeing the fields full of grain ready for harvest. He was extremely shy and hated school. He was not the one to fulfill Anthony's dream and once again Anthony was reminded of his personal failure.

His wife, Jenny, gave him three more children before she became too old for childbirth. They were all girls. Very bright, good children, but they were not able to fulfill his dream and calling. Many years passed and suddenly Jenny became pregnant. She wasn't supposed to be. She was too old. It was way too dangerous. But in spite of their fears, God gave them a son and they named him Robert. Robert and Henry didn't get along. Henry would do Robert's chores because Robert couldn't concentrate on what he was supposed to be doing. He was too busy socializing, talking, dreaming of impossible things, and preaching to the cows. Henry told him that if he couldn't make a living talking, he would starve.

Anthony made great sacrifices so Robert could go to school. He didn't buy shoes when he needed them; he lined the insides of his old shoes with cardboard to keep the snow out. He'd put another patch on his overalls rather than buy new ones. He bought the oldest farm equipment and kept it working with bailing wire.

Anthony walked in his own shoes. He fulfilled God's dream for his life. He did it with true humility, honor to God, love for his family, and a sacrificial spirit. Anthony was my grandfather.

CONTENTS

FOREWORD

I'm betting that I am much like you in that I certainly never expected to be walking in the shoes I'm in now. I had plans and dreams when I was young, but as is so often the case, life doesn't always seem to cooperate. I grew up so poor that sometimes there would be no food on the table if I didn't "collect" from the customers on my paper route. I was the only son of an alcoholic father who died too young. I made a lot of bad decisions when I was left to my own devices. And when I finally earned my PhD, that's when I discovered that I wasn't fulfilled as a clinical psychologist in private practice, a pretty disheartening reality when that had always been my big goal!

The list of unexpected turns in my life is endless, and I wasn't always sure where the journey would take me. The reason my life script changed more dramatically than I ever could have imagined is because God had other plans for me—just as He does for every single one of us.

Sure, I'd like to think that my hard work and determination to find my calling paid off, that the reason I'm on TV each day working to help people live better lives is because I feel in my heart that I have something important to say. But I can guarantee you that none of the blessings in my life would exist were it not for my faith in God and my firm belief that each of us can find a personal way to make a positive impact in this world.

I sure don't have all the answers, not for myself, and not for you. But I am fairly certain here that, like me, you have not had a success-only journey, but I do know this—as a child of God, you are on this earth as a unique individual, with a specific reason for being here.

You may have a vibrant, dynamic relationship with God or your faith may be rusty, but at this very moment, you are only pages away from looking at your life with a new point of view. Whether you've heard Dr. Robert A. Schuller, senior pastor of The Crystal Cathedral, on his "Hour of Power" broadcast, or if you are discovering this esteemed pastor for the first time, you are about to be inspired by a man whose steadfast faith is an example for us all. And whether you feel you've been dealt a bad hand or you're living with confidence and strength, *Walking In Your Own Shoes* will bring you closer to your true self and your ultimate purpose.

All too often, we feel weighed down by the baggage of our past. We are consumed by self-doubt, or we make an inevitable wrong turn with consequences that feel like a life sentence. With relatable analogies, insightful discoveries, and meaningful passages from Scripture, Dr. Schuller shows us how we can learn from our mistakes and assess who we are now so that we can partner with God as we move toward our future.

Walking in Your Own Shoes is made all the more powerful because Dr. Schuller includes very personal accounts of his life, growing up as the son of a preacher who found his own "shoes." He offers specific tools for creating a new definition of success in our lives, as well as learning to walk by faith.

God is at work in all of our lives, but sometimes we need a reminder that the obstacles in our path are not as big as they seem and that it is never too late to become His partner. Only when we let God in can we begin to live with purpose, and fulfill the promise He is asking us to fulfill. You've taken the first step by holding this book in your hands. It is my hope that you will enjoy the journey.

—Dr. Phil McGraw
Los Angeles, California
November 2007

ACKNOWLEDGMENTS

It takes many people dedicated to a common goal to write, produce, and market a successful book. So it is with this book. I want to begin by thanking my dear friends Foster and Lynn Friess. I was a guest in their home looking out over the valley at the Grand Tetons in Jackson Hole, Wyoming, when I wrote the thesis. That inspiration started everything. From there William Kruidenier helped me put my thoughts on paper. Without him they would still be running aimlessly through my brain without structure and composition.

The staff of Yates & Yates LLP, particularly Sealy Yates, and Jeana Ledbetter, created a formidable team with FaithWords of Hachette Book Group. Rolf Zettersten, senior vice president of Hachette Book Group and Gary Terashita, editor at Hachette Book Group, made it possible with their unique talents and gifts. Without the skills of the marketing efforts of the Crystal Cathedral staff and Hachette, the books would still be sitting on shelves in a warehouse somewhere. I want to give special mention to Jim Coleman and Mike Nason for their unique marketing ideas. They have continued through the years to be a great support for me and the Crystal Cathedral.

Dr. Phil McGraw has been a wonderful friend and counselor for my family and the Church. I am so blessed to have friends like him and his wife Robin. Thank you for writing the foreword.

I must give thanks for the commitment of the staff and leadership of the Crystal Cathedral for getting behind this book in every way. They gave me the time I needed to make it happen.

Finally, I could never forget my best friend and wife, Donna. She listens to all my complaints, ideas, and thoughts long before they ever get on paper. She corrects me when I need to hear the truth and comforts me when I need a soft loving touch. I thank God every day for my children, Angie, Bobby, Christina, and Anthony. They keep me humble and up to date. If it weren't for them I would be wearing the same clothes today I wore in the 70s. If they weren't the kids they are, I wouldn't be able to spend my mental energy in this positive direction.

INTRODUCTION

On Sunday morning, April 1, 2007, I dressed for church as usual: blue shirt, dark slacks, robe, and black leather "preacher" shoes—the same outfit I have donned for thousands of Sunday morning worship services over the past twenty-five years. Within a couple of hours, however, I discovered that, spiritually speaking, the shoes I had on that morning were not the ones best suited for the path I would travel that day. Had I known what was about to happen, I would probably have worn a pair of running shoes instead of my black leather ones. I was headed into unfamiliar territory.

My "territory" for the past twenty-five years (indeed, all my life as the son of a preacher) has been the Reformed Church in America (RCA). No one can trump the RCA in terms of history and tradition. Not only is the Reformed Church in America (formerly the Dutch Reformed Church) the oldest Protestant Christian denomination with continuous ministry in North America, it is the oldest corporation of any kind. It was our spiritual ancestors, members of the Dutch West India Company, who bought Manhattan from the Indians for the equivalent of twenty-four dollars in 1626. (Granted, it wasn't much—but for all concerned it seemed like a fair deal at the time.) The settlement of New Amsterdam and the Reformed Protestant Dutch Church would later birth itself from those original Dutch traders and settlers. The denomination's name was changed to the Reformed Church in America in 1867.

Most RCA churches in America are small in size—a few hundred members. The congregation my father, Dr. Robert H. Schuller, started in Garden Grove, California, in 1955 became the most non-traditional church in our denomination, as well as the largest. Holding the first services in a local drive-in movie theater was a non-traditional move itself. But ultimately building an all-glass "Crystal Cathedral" to host thousands of worshipers in multiple services on Sunday really set the church apart. The church became known around the world through the *Hour of Power* television program which broadcasts the Sunday services.

In spite of those innovations and my father's creative leadership, my background was RCA through and through—steeped in centuries of tradition. Before becoming senior pastor of the Crystal Cathedral in 2006, I started and pastored for twenty years an RCA congregation a few miles down the coast of California from my father's church. Inspired by my father's example, I attempted to find my own "shoes" in ministry. And the Lord blessed, touching the lives of many thousands of people in our community through our church, school, and other creative ministries.

But in all my years of pastoral ministry, nothing prepared me for what we experienced at the Crystal Cathedral that morning in April. Yes, it was April Fool's Day—but what happened was definitely not a joke.

As we often do on Sunday, we had a guest that morning my father was to interview about his spiritual life. These interviews through the years have been a highlight of the *Hour of Power* broadcasts. Guests have included politicians, business titans, athletes, individuals who have overcome great obstacles, members of the ministry, celebrities from the entertainment field, musicians—in other words, there is no restriction on who we will invite to be a part of our Sunday service. If God is at work in their life and their testimony can be an encouragement to our local and international broadcast congregations, we invite them to come.

Our guest that morning was a well-known celebrity, an international entertainer now retired from his rather strenuous, travel-based lifestyle. For decades he was known as a hard-living, hard-playing, flamboyant Las Vegas–style entertainer whose larger-than-life reputation was no exaggeration. But in recent years God had been at work in his life. He found salvation in Jesus Christ and was more than ready to give testimony to that experience when he visited our church.

Normally, the guest interviews are brief. But our guest that morning was so emboldened, I believe by the Holy Spirit, that my father didn't even get to interview our guest as intended; instead, when Evel Knievel—that's right, Evel Knievel—was introduced, he stepped into the pulpit and preached for fifteen minutes! He was passionate, articulate, and moving as he declared what God had done in his life. Our congregation was hanging on every word, and I could see people dabbing at their eyes throughout the church as this formerly hard-living man became like a child telling about the love of Jesus.

As the logical, and theological, conclusion to his remarks, he turned to my father and said he needed, and wanted, to be baptized—right there, that morning. It reminded me of the Ethiopian official in Acts 8 who asked Philip, "Look, here is water. Why shouldn't I be baptized?" (v. 36). Why not, indeed! And Robert Evel Knievel was baptized. There wasn't a dry eye in the place.

As most churches whose Sunday services are destined for broadcast on television, ours are scripted to the minute. But God was changing our script. It was time for me to collect the offering and then preach. But the offering seemed totally out of place. I also realized we had already seen and heard the best sermon we could have hoped for. Anything I might add would have been anti-climactic at best. Besides, I believed the Lord was saying something different to me: I knew there must be others who wanted to be baptized after seeing and hearing Evel. So I decided to give an invitation for anyone who wanted to be baptized to come forward and be baptized right then and there.

What happened next was completely unexpected. They came by the hundreds! It was the most amazing experience of my ministerial life.

As do most churches in the Reformed tradition, we normally baptize by sprinkling rather than immersion, though we do both. We put the emphasis on meaning, not means. When our pastors saw how many were coming to be baptized, four of them also took a bowl of water and began helping me baptize them all. People were crying tears of joy as they professed their faith and received the sacrament of baptism. I was crying, the other pastors were crying—we were baptizing with salt water after a while. Five pastors were baptizing people as fast as we could for thirty minutes!

And that was just in the first service. In the second service, the same thing happened: same guest, same testimony, same response, same invitation, and same baptisms of multitudes of people. As best we can figure, we think nearly eight hundred people were baptized that Sunday morning. Many of them were Christians who had put off attending our new-member class which culminates in baptism. And many of them were non-churched folks from the community who came to hear our guest speak. I'm confident scores, maybe hundreds, of people were born again that morning as a result of Evel Knievel's powerful testimony.

Do you see now why I said I should have worn running shoes, or trail boots, instead of my traditional black leather shoes? This was not a normal church service at the Crystal Cathedral or in any congregation in the Reformed Church in America. As I write these words I am still reflecting on that marvelous morning. I fully expect that God is going to use what happened to speak to us about our past, present, and future as a church; to give us new insight about the kind of walking shoes we're going to need to do what He calls us to do in the future.

There is no one I admire more than my father, Robert H. Schuller. Yet when I succeeded him as the senior pastor of the Crystal Cathedral I knew I was not going to merely step into his shoes. I knew God had different shoes for me. He always does! And that is the message of the book you are about to read: how do we gain the courage, the maturity, the insight, and the knowledge from God to become our own person—the person He created us to be?

It's so easy to live our lives in the shadow of others—a parent, a mentor, or someone whose esteem we greatly value. Yes, we can honor them and learn from them and respect their impact on our lives, but we are not them! We are individual and unique bearers of the image of God in whom and through whom God wants to do something never done before. If we are ever going to experience all of who He is and all of who He created us to be, we're going to have to learn to trust Him—to stand in awe and amazement at what He can do when we least expect it. And that's what this book is about.

It's about the journey—the path, the walk—that each of us is on in this life. It's about finding the shoes that fit us and no one else—a lifestyle of faith rooted in a sovereign, unpredictable, but trustworthy God who has called us to Himself for our good and His glory. It's about being willing to move beyond the traditional and safe harbors in which we live our lives, believing God has something that needs doing in this world only we can do.

Why do we keep falling into the trap of thinking we are not good enough to be used by God to make a powerful impact in the world? We allow negative thoughts and critical behavior training to highlight all of our own faults and weaknesses instead of accentuating the positive. In spite of our sins and shortcomings, God wants to use us!

The Bible is filled with people God used who, by today's standards of ability and nobility, wouldn't have qualified for much at all. Noah was a drunk, Abraham was too old, Isaac was a daydreamer, Jacob was a liar, Joseph was abused, Moses stuttered, Gideon was afraid, Samson was a womanizer, Rahab was a prostitute, Jeremiah was too young, David was an adulterer, Elisha was suicidal, Isaiah preached naked, Jonah ran from God, Naomi was a widow, Job went bankrupt, John the Baptist ate bugs, Peter denied Christ, all of the disciples fell asleep while praying, Martha worried about everything, the Samaritan woman had several failed marriages, Zacchaeus was too small, Paul was too religious, Timothy was too young and had ulcers, and Lazarus was dead.

If God had something He wanted those individuals to do, then there is something He wants you and me to do as well. We just have to be willing to be shown what it is and then go for it!

I hope you'll read this book prayerfully, asking God with each page, "Speak to me, Lord. Open my eyes. Help me see the walking shoes You have for me. I am ready to follow where You lead." Don't pray that prayer casually—God will answer. You can either say no when He shows you what to do, or you can grab the water and start baptizing. I heartily recommend the latter!

Walking in Your Own Shoes

God has created every
individual to be unique.
Every person has what
he or she needs to
succeed in life.

Designed for the Journey

His divine power has given us everything we need for life and godliness through our knowledge of him who called us by his own glory and goodness. Through these he has given us his very great and precious promises, so that through them you may participate in the divine nature and escape the corruption in the world caused by evil desires.

—2 Peter 1:3–4

Randall Bingham IV loved coming home from college at winter semester break. But this Christmas his anticipation was bordering on intimidation based on a decision he had recently made.

The traditional Christmas Eve gathering for the Bingham clan, hosted in his parents' spacious and sumptuous home, was an annual pass-in-review for himself, his siblings, and his cousins. Over the years it had become the way for the elder Binghams—grandfather Randall "the second" plus his son and sons-in-law—to assess the progress and performance of the rising generations. By the time the evening was over, every young person in the family had been informally interviewed as to present progress and future plans. It was this family muster that had Randall more than a little worried.

In New England, "Bingham" was a synonym for "attorney." In Randall's case, since his father was the senior partner of the family law firm begun by his great-grandfather, it had been understood that the legal mantle was Randall's to inherit. Graduating from college, then on to an Ivy League law school—the script had been in place for as long as he could remember.

He had avoided detailed interrogation up until the time the family was seated for dinner—high schoolers and up at one massive table, everyone else at tables in an adjoining room. As service of the formal meal began, Randall's uncle Charles opened the questioning.

"So, Randall," Charles began, "you're halfway through your junior year. Have you narrowed down the list of law schools you're going to apply to?"

"Not yet, Uncle Charles," Randall began, focusing on the peas he was serving himself instead of looking up to see how many of the eighteen pairs of eyes at the table were actually focused on him. "I'm definitely giving it a lot of thought, though—and prayer!" He looked up and smiled at that—it couldn't hurt to get God in his corner for what was to come.

"Well, that's good—that's good," Charles responded, with a "what's there to pray about?" tone in his voice. "Tell us what you're considering."

"Well, actually, things have been so busy since I got home that I haven't even had a chance to talk about this with Mom and Dad—so I probably ought to wait to fill you in until after I've talked with them."

The conversation at the table dropped noticeably with that statement, which Randall tried to restart by asking that the gravy boat be passed his way. But he knew his father, at one end of the table, and his mother, at the other end, were focused not on gravy but on the possible crack in the foundation of the future of one Randall Edwards Bingham IV.

"Go ahead, Randall," his father said, laying down his knife and fork and leaning forward, elbows on the table. "We're all family here. Tell us what you're thinking."

Randall could either lie ("I've been thinking about medical school instead of law school") and allow the meal to recover with just a speed bump, or tell the truth and create a train wreck. No time like the present, he reasoned.

"Well, I've been thinking about not going directly to law school after I graduate." Suddenly you could hear the ice melting in the crystal water glasses.

Randall continued. "Through the campus student-ministry organization I'm involved with at school I've been learning about some incredible possibilities to get involved overseas—some underdeveloped parts of the world. The needs are so huge—literacy, health, business and economic development, agriculture, legal injustice—it's amazing! When I think about the way God has wired me—the things that are important to me and what I'm good at—and *where I might have the opportunity to do the most good with my life, I've been thinking it might be in a setting like that as opposed to being an attorney here.*

"Here's what I'm thinking," he continued. "I'd do a summer internship overseas this coming summer, spend my senior year narrowing the alternatives, then graduate and spend one to two years working overseas. If it works out and I see I'm making a difference, and decide I need further education, say a medical degree, I'd return and go back to school before going back on a permanent basis, say, as a medical missionary."

There's no telling how long the silence at the table would have lasted if Randall's tenth-grade cousin, Shelly, hadn't piped up. "A missionary?" she said, voicing what everyone was thinking. Or maybe not: "That'd be awesome!"

Maybe God was in his corner after all.

Y OU COULD PROBABLY CHANGE a few details and make that story apply to you at some point in your life journey. I have heard numerous theme variations as I have counseled and prayed with individuals seeking to find their path in life, often trying to overcome the expectations of family, loved ones, or friends. The challenge to find and fulfill one's own calling in life is perhaps our most important task.

Hopefully all of us are having a running dialogue with God in prayer about finding our own path in life; about finding our own shoes to walk in—shoes that feel more and more comfortable the further we walk in them.

It's a lifelong conversation, a self-talk mature people have with themselves all their lives. Personally, I have not yet put a period at the end of that conversation in my own life, and I don't anticipate doing so. Life is a journey, not a destination, and the path of our individuality and uniqueness in God's sight will continue to unfold as long as we live.

Why are we so inclined to walk in others' shoes instead of our own? It's because we don't think we have what we need to succeed. For some reason, we think everyone else in life got what they needed but we didn't. We think God intended for us to be followers, not leaders; dependent, not independent; traditional, not creative; fearful, not courageous; static, not changing; safe, not risky; walking in a rut, not blazing a new trail.

Wrong! God intends each of us to have the resources and confidence we need to choose what to do and who to become in our lives. We may need training or information or money or advice. But those are the easy things to get compared to what holds most people back: the ability to believe God created them and equipped them to be unique and significant.

There is no greater feeling in the world than when we realize we are doing something we've never done before—something we thought we'd never be able to do. I've witnessed three out of four of my children coming face-to-face with this reality as they learned to ride two-wheel bikes. (The fourth, before his third birthday, just hopped on and took off as if he was born to ride.) As all parents do, I would run alongside the children with my hands on the bike seat, keeping them steady. Up and down the street we'd go as the children gradually gained confidence. Occasionally, without telling the child, I would take my hands off the seat and allow them to ride increasing distances on their own, running alongside with my hands out of sight. They would think I was holding on, that it was me keeping them from falling.

Eventually, when I was confident they didn't need me any longer I would run a few feet ahead and show my child my hands. For a split second there would be a wobble and a look of confusion. I could tell the neurons were firing by the billions in their little brains as they tried to compute the fact they were riding without me holding them up. And then it would click! Their faces would break out in sheer joy as they realized they were riding with "no hands"—at least, without my hands. *They were now free to go wherever they wanted on a bike.*

Even as adults, we have those moments in life where we are caught between the sheer terror of falling and the sheer ecstasy of staying upright. God "shows us His hands" to let us know we're actually on our own, and we scream, "Put your hands back on the bike! Catch me! Hold me!" We have a hard time believing He has trained us (equipped us) thoroughly enough to break free and go wherever we want in life.

But recall Peter's words: "[God's] divine power has given us everything we need for life and godliness through Christ." Our challenge is to believe those words; to look in the mirror and say, "God has provided everything I need for life and godliness."

Believing the world was round was hard for tho[se] it was flat. Believing the earth revolved around those who always believed the opposite. It take[s] change our minds about serious issues in life. T[...] you six categories of evidence that should encourage you to believe God has given you everything you need to live and achieve your dreams.

Think of the following six realities like stages progressing upward from the broad base of a pyramid to the point at the top—and you are the point!

God's Existence: Presence

This point is the broadest and simplest of all: If God exists and is a presence in the universe, the possibilities in life are endless. If God doesn't exist—if life as we know it is the result of the continual and accidental collision of matter—then little of consequence, individually or otherwise, is worth pursuing.

The November 2006 issue of *Wired* magazine—regarded as a bible among high-tech types for having its finger on the pulse of forward-thinking trends—featured a cover story titled "The Church of the Non-Believers." The byline of the article read, "A band of intellectual brothers is mounting a crusade against belief in God. Are they winning converts, or merely preaching to the choir?" The article detailed the efforts of three well-known atheists, all highly respected in their fields of philosophy and science, to promote disbelief in the existence of God.

I can only say I would hate to be in their shoes. The vast majority of the world's population believes in God. I don't mean Jesus Christ as God, but God as a being who exists—the opposite of what atheists believe. To use the title of a book written by the late theologian Francis Schaeffer, most people believe "God is there and He is not silent."

Think about what it feels like to drive up to a darkened building at night where you're supposed to meet someone. It can feel off, disconcerting, even scary. You call out, "Hello—anybody home?" Suddenly a light comes on and a familiar face appears around a corner: "Sorry—I just got here. Come on back to the office. I'm glad you're here." Relief! The idea of not being alone is a powerful force.

at's the difference it makes that God exists. Instead of being met
th cold silence when we speak into the universe with a tentative, "Anybody home?" God speaks, letting us know we are not alone.

The difference God's presence makes is simply this: you and I are
not left to our own devices in this life. God is big and He is present and
He is able to provide everything we need to live the creative, strong, and
independent lives we desire.

I have been asked more than once, "Who have been some of the most
influential people in your life?" There have been many, but one I'll never
forget is Ray Beckering, who appeared on the *Hour of Power* broadcast
when it first began, reading the Scriptures and praying. As a young man
I would listen to him and long to know how to pray like he did. When I
asked him to teach me to pray, he said, "The first thing you have to do
is realize to whom you are praying." In other words, who is God to you?
Our prayers reflect the idea of God we carry in our mind. Our prayers
manifest the impact God has made in our lives.

God's Ability: Sovereignty

You may remember an experiment begun in 1984 called Biosphere 2.
It was an attempt to set up an enclosed and self-sustaining living environment—a microcosm of life on earth: plants producing oxygen and
food, water, soil, animals, and insects. The biosphere was a three-plus-
acre airtight world where eight "bionauts" were to live completely independent of the outside world.

Unfortunately, they discovered that man's sovereignty over his own
existence was pretty limited. Despite $200 million invested from 1984
to 1991 to build the biosphere, a multimillion-dollar annual operating
budget, and almost unlimited technical support from contributing gov-
ernmental and scientific agencies, Biosphere 2 was a failure. They found
it was impossible to sustain the lives of the eight participants over the
planned two-year course of the experiment.

Just sixteen months after the eight participants were sealed inside in
1991, oxygen levels had to be supplemented from outside. Nineteen of
twenty-five vertebrate species became extinct. The pollinating species
went extinct, meaning the vegetation couldn't reproduce and bear food.

And water and air pollution became uncontrollable. Man's best efforts to gain control over his environment proved to be unsuccessful after a little more than one year.

Contrast the failure of Biosphere 2 with "Biosphere 1"—the planet-home we call earth. Our self-contained, self-sustaining planet, that draws its life-giving energy from the sun, continues to re-create and heal itself in spite of all the goop and grime man has released into the system. That's not an invitation for us to live with license and disregard for our planet, but a testament to its amazing ability to support life. Clearly there is a big difference between man's "sovereignty" and God's.

There is a powerful life-force at work in our world, and His name is God. Our planet is not a cosmic pinball machine with you and me playing the parts of ball bearings bouncing from one post to the other. God created this world and sustains it for a purpose. And you are part of that purpose. You play a significant role in God's sovereign plan for this world.

God's Love: Relationship

At this point, let's take a significant step toward personalizing what God has done for *you*—from deism to theism. A deist is someone who believes in a God who created the universe but then abandoned it, much like a watchmaker who builds a watch, winds it up, then allows it to run down without interference from him. That's what some believe the God who created our world has done—put it in motion and then stepped back, allowing it to take its own course.

How comforting is that idea to someone seeking to live to his or her fullest potential? It's the equivalent of a father bringing a child into the world and saying, "Good luck—you're on your own now!" The idea of not having a relationship with the God who created us is depressing at best and defeating at worst.

Fortunately, the Bible gives us a totally different picture of God. The Bible says God is love (see 1 John 4:8, 16) and that He acts accordingly. From the very beginning of the human story the Bible pictures God interacting with and providing for mankind (see Gen. 3:8). Ultimately, God's intimate and personal love for man was revealed when He came to earth in the person of Jesus, His Son. John 3:16, the most famous verse in the Bible, says God loved us so much He came to earth to meet with us and provide what we need to live life. Jesus Himself said, "I came so they can have real and eternal life, more and better life than they ever dreamed of" (John 10:10 The Message).

Think about that. Whatever life you have dreamed about having, Jesus came to provide it and more. I'm sure these words of Jesus are what inspired the apostle Paul (who discovered a life better than he had ever imagined) to write, "Now glory be to God! By his mighty power at work within us, he is able to accomplish infinitely more than we would ever dare to ask or hope" (Eph. 3:20 NLT).

If we expect to build a life of stability, strength, power, goodness, and quality, it is imperative we start with the right spiritual foundation. Any life built on a foundation other than Jesus Christ is a life built on sand—a life that will fall when the storms come against it. But when we build a life on the foundation of Christ we can build beauty and strength into it over the long term—little by little, year by year. Such a building becomes a relationship that guards us against the storms inevitably to arise. God has not promised we won't go through storms, but He has promised He will go through them with us.

God's Creation: Humanity

So out of His very essence, which is love, God created you. He put you in a world that would sustain you and even came to earth in person to introduce Himself and meet your deepest spiritual needs. And He gave you something else: others.

Sadly, too many people live in a personal world of intimate strangers. It was never intended by God to be that way as evidenced by His second recorded conversation with the first man. Adam's first assignment from God was to name all the animals created, a task which left him in an unenviable position: he was the solitary soul on planet Earth. Every other being on planet Earth with a face had another face like its own to look at, another pair of eyes to meet in some measure of shared meaning.

But not Adam. So God's second conversation with His earthly, human gardener was to tell him it wasn't good for him to be alone. And not just for procreative purposes either. It wasn't *healthy* for Adam to be alone. Without a partner he would not have learned to talk, to discuss, to debate, to plan, to compromise, or to give and receive advice, correction, and exhortation. In short, Adam never would have blossomed or reached his full potential without another human being.

The turbulent 1960s in America billed itself as the decade of "free love," but produced a lot of pained people. Paul Simon, the songwriting half of the folk-pop duo Simon and Garfunkel, spoke for a lot of frustrated free-lovers when he wrote the song, "I Am a Rock." First released in 1965, the song's voice says, "I've built walls, a fortress deep and mighty, that none may penetrate. I have no need of friendship; friendship causes pain. It's laughter and it's loving I disdain. I am a rock, I am an island."

Whether Simon's words are autobiographical or not, they are still painful to hear. Yet the reality is many have closed themselves off to the rest of the human race. All of us would be better off heeding the words of the English poet John Donne who wrote, "No man is an island, entire of itself." All are connected, Donne went on to write, all are part of the whole of humanity.

God has given you family and friends to help shape you, encourage you, strengthen you, sharpen you, and draw you out onto the path that is right for you. Humanity is God's gift to itself.

In our high-tech world we need to become a high-touch people, a philosophy espoused at a cancer treatment center called Commonweal. At Commonweal patients are helped to uncover any underlying emotional conditions that may block the body's natural healing processes, such as bitterness or anger.

A Holocaust survivor named Yatsik came to the center from Czechoslovakia and discovered that hugging was a fundamental therapy employed—something he was not used to and with which he was not entirely comfortable. Commonweal is a high-touch healing environment, using hugging and other therapeutic forms of touch to establish bonds of love and acceptance.

After his initial reluctance Yatsik became more comfortable with being hugged. By day four he was participating in the daily times of morning prayer and meditation. He asked God in prayer, "God, is it okay to reach out and touch strangers? To accept a hug from somebody I don't know?" In his prayers he heard the response of God: "Strangers? What is a stranger? I never created strangers."

For Yatsik it was a turning point. He was able to break through the fear of not getting close to anyone. His Holocaust experience caused him to view the world with fear and distrust. But being hugged and loved by fellow human beings was the beginning of emotional healing for him. A smile, a hug, the commitment of love—these are powerful healing tools in our lives.

God's Household: Church

The triangle gets even narrower now. Within the family of humanity there is an even closer-knit band of kindred spirits God gives to those who know Him in Christ—His church.

There were not always two groups of human beings—those who know God personally and those who don't. For a fleeting moment in history every single human being on planet Earth loved God—all two of them. Before Adam and Eve chose to disobey God's commands they enjoyed an intimate relationship with Him. The whole human family was one with God.

But after they disobeyed God, they and all their descendants had to make a conscious choice to return to fellowship with Him. As it stands now, those who have made that choice through His Son, Jesus Christ, are called His church—the fellowship of believers. If you are a Christian you have been united in spirit by the Holy Spirit of God with all other believers who share your faith. You are not only "in Christ," you are also in the body of Christ. And that is a powerful thing God has done for you.

The phrase "one another" is used seventy-five times in the New Testament (NIV). That is emblematic of the amazing reality that exists among people who are united by their faith. "Me" and "mine" have been replaced by "we" and "our." When one person rejoices, all rejoice; when one weeps, all weep (see 1 Cor. 12:26).

And when you need guidance on your path, your faith-family is there to speak the wisdom of God to you; to pray with you; to counsel you; to correct you; to affirm you. The wisdom of Proverbs says there is a friend who sticks closer than a brother, and these are the friends it is referring to—friends with whom you share your faith (see Prov. 18:24).

In January 1984 I announced to the congregation I was then pastoring that I was soon to experience a divorce from my wife. I viewed that church service as a funeral; I thought my ministry was over.

I had no idea how the congregation would respond to my words. After finishing my remarks I sat down with my head bowed, staring at the floor. Within seconds I heard the sound of footsteps coming toward me, and I looked up to discover almost the entire congregation joining me on the platform behind the pulpit. They came to affirm their love for me and to assure me my ministry was not over. With God, sometimes what seems like an ending is more often just a new beginning.

My church family held me up in what was the most difficult moment of my life as a person and a pastor. Their strength convinced me I could survive. And they were right.

God's Image: You!

Finally, the tip of the pyramid—the thin edge of the wedge: You! You are that unique individual God created in His own image and gifted with resources and abilities to live a life reflecting His glory.

A speaker began his seminar by holding up a twenty-dollar bill and asking who in the room was interested in having it. Of course, almost every hand went up. "I'm going to give it to one of you as soon as I do this . . ." he said—whereupon he wadded the bill into a tiny ball and rolled it around between his palms.

"Anybody still want it now?" he asked the audience. And the same hands went up.

"Okay, what if I do this?" he said, dropping the wadded-up bill on the floor and dramatically stomping it with his foot and grinding it into the carpet beneath his shoe. "Anybody still want this badly treated twenty-dollar bill now?" he asked. Again, all the hands went up.

The speaker's point became obvious to his audience. The value of the twenty-dollar bill was not dependent on its being wrinkle-free or in nearly new condition. The value of the bill was based on the images on the face of it: the signs and seals of the U.S. Treasury; the signature of the Secretary of the Treasury; the numerical dollar amounts in the corners. That's what made the twenty-dollar bill valuable, not its condition.

And that's what makes you valuable. The greatest resource you have is not your environment, your fellow human beings, the church, or your own gifts and abilities. It is the image of God you bear for His glory. God created you to be just as fulfilled as He. He created you to be like Him.

Dr. Norman Vincent Peale is one of my heroes. His 1952 book *The Power of Positive Thinking* is one of the greatest books ever written, still widely read today. When my father began what is now the Crystal Cathedral in a drive-in movie theater, Dr. Peale came and spoke to an overflowing crowd, giving that church planting effort a boost of energy from the very start.

I was around ten years old when I heard Dr. Peale tell a story that became a favorite of my father's—and mine. Dr. Peale was in Hong Kong and walked into a tattoo shop where he looked at the myriad images and designs from which customers could choose to have drawn on their bodies. He saw the traditional "Born to Lose" design and asked the shop owner, "Sir, do people actually want 'Born to Lose' tattooed on their bodies? Why?"

The owner replied, "Sir, before that is tattooed on their bodies, it is already tattooed on their minds."

That is definitely not the message of the gospel of Jesus Christ. The powerful transformation that occurs in a person's life when he or she comes to know Christ changes "Born to Lose" to "Born to Succeed." Children of God have been called for a purpose—and that purpose is to win, not to lose. If you and I will tattoo "I am a child of God" on our minds every day, that is what we will become in our attitudes and our actions.

John 1:12 says "To those who believed in [Christ's] name, he gave the right to become children of God." The word "right" means power and authority, and therefore means by believing in Christ we are given power and authority to live as God's child. And that means power and authority to succeed in accomplishing that which God has put in our hearts to do. That's why Peter says, "His divine power has given us everything we need for life and godliness through our knowledge of him who called us by his own glory and goodness" (2 Pet. 1:3). If you are God's child through faith in Christ you have been given everything you need.

Every person's experiences
in life are unique. God
uses the journey itself to
reveal more and more of
our unique identities.

Designed by the Journey

When Pharaoh let the people go, God did not lead them on the road through the Philistine country, though that was shorter. For God said, "If they face war, they might change their minds and return to Egypt." So God led the people around by the desert road toward the Red Sea. The Israelites went up out of Egypt armed for battle.

—Exodus 13:17–18

Nicole slumped into a chair in Professor Sheldon's cramped office. While she waited for him to arrive for their meeting, she looked around at the lifetime's worth of stuff filling the room. Books, of course, from floor to ceiling, more than the shelves were designed to hold. Pictures scattered around in frames—his wife, children, and grandchildren she assumed. Degrees, certificates, and awards leaning against the wall in a corner on the floor. She wasn't surprised. Dr. Sheldon wasn't the type to toot his own horn.

And the archaeological artifacts—stuck in every nook and cranny in the bookcases. Oil lamps, coins, stones with inscriptions. It suddenly hit her as strange that she was coming to get counsel about her life from a professor of archaeology. But he was old and wise and seemed to know things not in books.

Her thoughts were interrupted by Dr. Sheldon opening the door and shuffling into his office. She immediately knew why she liked him. She felt like she was about to talk to the grandfather she always wanted but never had.

Nicole was confused about her life—where she was and where she was headed. She wasn't sure she belonged at a Bible college but didn't have a better alternative. Her broken home left her insecure and fearful of commitments with people. She worked hard at a couple of different jobs to pay for school, which left her little time for socializing. Her faith was intact, though she often wondered why God seemed not to be closer to her. She felt she was traveling her road alone.

"Nicole," Dr. Sheldon began, after listening patiently to her talk for a while, "you're telling my story. You're singing my song. Did you know that I sometimes feel the way you are feeling right now? And I certainly felt that way when I was your age."

"Dr. Sheldon, how is that possible? I mean, you seem like you have it all together. That's why I came to talk to you."

"Well, don't let my age and my steady job fool you, my dear," the professor said with a smile. "Sometimes I think that after seventy-one years I should have it all together. But I've concluded we never really do. This thing called life is a road full of twists and turns. We never know where the next roadblock will be or what will be around the next bend. That was unsettling for me when I was your age, and it still is to a degree now. But I have learned this: God uses both the certainties and the uncertainties of life to mold us into the people He wants us to become. You're in one of those uncertain places right now, but it's no less a part of the journey than the certain places."

"What kind of uncertain places have you been in?—if you don't mind my asking," Nicole said, sitting up a little straighter in her chair.

"Not at all, not at all," he said, turning to look out the window, like he was looking back down the road of his life. The professor walked Nicole through the ups and downs of his life giving example after example of how he recognized, after the fact, that God used people, events, his failures more than his successes, even his sins, to shape his life. "I've learned you don't get from point A to point D without going through B and C. But while you're passing through B and C it's hard to see the point. But they're all part of the journey.

"I remember in my studies coming across this passage in Exodus that tells how God led the children of Israel out of their slavery in Egypt on a huge

detour through the desert so they wouldn't encounter the Philistines and be defeated just a few days after gaining their freedom. That was a huge 'Aha!' moment for me. It told me God sees what's ahead on the road even when I can't."

Nicole sat silently, so the professor concluded: "Because you're twenty-one and I'm seventy-one, I may have this one thing together a bit better than you: Life is a journey, the future points of which only God knows. But because He knows, we can trust that He is leading us exactly where we need to be—one step at a time."

I N 1861, A FRENCH ENGINEER named Charles Joseph Minard drew a very strange-looking graphic. It was roughly two feet wide and a foot and a half tall and consisted of a colored band flowing like a jagged river from left to right, decreasing in size, then turning and flowing back across the page from right to left, arriving at its starting point a tiny fraction of the size at which it began. There are date stamps along the way, connected by vertical lines to a chart of temperature readings across the bottom of the page. Strange as it looks, Edward Tufte, professor emeritus of statistics and design at Yale, says Minard's work is the best statistical graph ever drawn.

When one studies Minard's *Carte Figurative*, its meaning unfolds. It is a graphic portrayal of the losses of the French army in the Russian campaign of 1812–1813. Napoleon's journey from France to Moscow was a defining event in the French emperor-general's life.

Napoleon left Europe in June 1812 intending to force Tsar Alexander I to submit to Napoleon's rule, with more than a half million soldiers from France and other conquered regions—the largest army ever assembled under the command of one man. (This number was represented by the thick end of Minard's "river.") By the end of the year more than 98 percent of Napoleon's massive army was dead; only ten thousand managed to make it back to France. (This was represented by the sliver end of the graphic, ending where it began.) Russia was unconquered and Napoleon was humiliated and exiled to the island of Elba. Unable to gain a clear-cut victory over the Russians, Napoleon's army was caught in retreat by a horrific winter. Those not killed in battle starved or froze to death. And Charles Minard captured the whole thing on a single sheet of paper. (You can view Minard's graphic map of a year in Napoleon's life at Edward Tufte's Web site: www.edwardtufte.com/tufte/posters.)

We might say Charles Minard created a life-map of a year in the life of Napoleon Bonaparte and his army. It shows the journey from France to Moscow and back and the terrible downsizing of the French army and the impact of the winter. It was not a good year for Napoleon. He abdicated his throne in 1814, but staged a hundred-day comeback from exile that ended in his defeat by a coalition of armies at the Battle of Waterloo in 1815. Minard's graphic shows that we never know what our life's journey will look like and how it will define us. Napoleon was never the same after 1812.

All of us have bad years—or months or weeks or days. All of us end up thinner emotionally, spiritually, even physically after going through certain parts of our journey than when we began. Some counselors have incorporated the idea of a life-map into their practice, actually having counselees chart the ups and downs of their life on paper. A life-map could cover the whole of one's life or a certain segment. Like Minard's graphic, it provides a bird's-eye view of a period of time allowing connections to be seen and insights to be gained.

A life-map might allow a person to note that his gradual drift away from spiritual things began not long after his parents' divorce. Or it might allow a person to note that a chronic medical condition could be related to an emotionally traumatic experience. Whether those kinds of specific connections are made or not, a life-map allows us to accomplish something we rarely do: look at life as a journey. While we can't see into the future, we can see the past and present—and we can even extrapolate into the future based on those experiences.

In the previous chapter I said God designed you *for* the journey of your life—a kind of horizontal, or linear, view of God having equipped you with everything necessary to go forward and accomplish your dreams. But in this chapter I want to say God designs you *by* the journey as well—a vertical cross-section look at the individual experiences and times of your life and how God uses them to shape us.

It is often said our experiences in life can make us either bitter or better. If we allow God into those experiences and learn to find and apply His message to us, we will invariably become better. In that way we are designed *by* our journey through this life.

And what does "better" mean? In an overall sense, it means what the apostle Paul said in Romans 8:29: "For those God foreknew he also predestined to be conformed to the likeness of his Son." There's the goal—to be as mature, stable, holy, and fruitful as Jesus Himself. Our life is a journey leading to Christlikeness. And from the perspective of the journey itself the Bible provides a pair of bookends which give us confidence about the past and future of that journey.

One of the most powerful verses in the Bible addresses the future. David wrote Psalm 139 as a meditation on the all-knowing nature of God. He wanted God to search his heart and see if there was anything less than true devotion to be found there (see vv. 23–24). And he knew God could do that because God is everywhere and knows everything. A corollary to God's omniscience (His all-knowingness) is found in verse 16: "All the days ordained for me were written in your book before one of them came to be."

One of the things David was convinced God knew about him was the span of his life—the number and content of his days. I won't read more into that interpretation than is reasonable in terms of the degree to which God plans even the minutest details of our lives for the goal of our maturity. But I believe we can rest in the fact God knows our future—the ups and the downs of our journey through life.

From the point of view of the past we can rest in Romans 8:28: "And we know that in all things God works for the good of those who love him, who have been called according to his purpose." Whether God has planned all the events of our lives or not, we know God can use them for the good of those who have been called to become like Jesus (see v. 29).

So looking forward, God knows all the days of our lives before they ever come to pass. And looking back, God uses all the days of our lives to accomplish the goal of our becoming like Jesus. And I can't imagine anyone being dissatisfied with the opportunity to be like Him—purposeful, attractive, joyful, and fruitful.

There are six aspects of our journey through life that can help define who we are. But that increased sense of definition comes only to those who will study and stay closely attuned to the journey of their lives. Our Life-Journey is similar to a vacation journey in that the slower we go, the more questions we ask; and the more open we are to discovery, the more valuable the trip.

As you consider the following six dimensions of your Life-Journey, keep this idea of Solomon in mind: gaining insight is like "a prospector panning for gold, like an adventurer on a treasure hunt" (Prov. 2:4 The Message). You are the gold and the treasure! As you search for the person God made, and is making you to be, go slowly, ask questions, and be ready to receive what He shows you.

Journeys Have a Past

In the 1950s, nutritionist and author Adelle Davis created great controversy in health circles by declaring, "You are what you eat." Her views are now more widely accepted as the link between health and nutrition has been firmly established. Following Adelle Davis we can apply the same link to who we are today: we are the sum total of every physical, spiritual, and emotional experience we have ever had. In other words, journeys have a past we ignore at our own peril.

The theme of this book is that God has given you and me unique shoes to walk in on our journey through life. And no one—I repeat, *no one*—has shoes like yours. Why? Because no one's past is exactly like yours.

Since grammar school we have known that no two snowflakes are alike. But what most of us didn't learn is why. And the answer is it's all about the journey. In other words, like us, snowflakes are designed *by* the journey they take. Also like us, all snowflakes are the same in some ways. Specifically, they are all hexagonal—they have six arms arising from a six-sided central crystal. But the way they express their "six-sidedness" is unique for each one. As a tiny droplet of water turns to ice and begins to fall from and through clouds in the atmosphere, it passes through constantly varying conditions. The combination of temperature, air pressure, and humidity are minutely, or drastically, different at every level of the atmosphere. As a result, the hexagonal shape of every snow-flake grows differently on its journey to earth.

While we honor the forces of nature that make every snowflake and every grain of sand different, we have a harder time honoring the "forces" in our past that have made us who we are today. I repeat: no one has a past like yours. The more you know about the previous stages of your journey, the more insightful you will be about the present.

Honor your past! Regardless of how painful or pleasant, God has over-seen every step of your journey and will use it to prepare you for today and tomorrow.

Journeys Have a Present

The past I just encouraged you to honor is going to be different twenty-four hours from now. By tomorrow, the life you are living today is going to be part of your past. It is going to be part of that ever-increasing reservoir of experiences and knowledge you will draw on when you step into the future.

I couldn't possibly count the number of times I have heard or read advice about "leaving the past behind." We're told today is a brand-new day—it's the first day of the rest of your life. I'm sure I've said and written those words myself, and in a way they're accurate. Even the apostle Paul said, after becoming a Christian, that everything in his past was "rubbish"—that he had to "press on" into the future, leaving the past behind (Philippians 3:8, 12). I understand what Paul was saying. Once his eyes were opened by Christ, everything he deemed important in the past seemed inconsequential.

But think of this: without all the years of rabbinical training in the Scriptures, sitting at the feet of Gamaliel, one of Israel's most learned rabbis (see Acts 22:3), how would Paul have been able to write so eloquently and convincingly about the present? When we read Romans, Galatians, and Ephesians, and marvel at Paul's integration of the old covenant and the new, we forget that what we are reading is the integration of his past with his present.

The richer you can make today, the more useful it will be to you tomorrow when it is part of your past. When the Latin poet Horace wrote the words (*Odes* 1.11) *carpe diem*—"seize the day!"—he did it in the sense of "eat, drink, and be merry," or "grab all the gusto you can." I prefer to find profit in his words by focusing on today as a way to prepare for tomorrow.

Even better advice than *carpe diem* is *carpe Deus*—"seize God!" Asking Him daily for wisdom and insight and direction is the best way I know to make the present a firm foundation for tomorrow.

When you get out of bed tomorrow morning, you can choose to say reluctantly, "Oh dear God, it's morning." Or you can express your love to Almighty God by choosing the positive attitude and saying, "This is the day God has made. I will be glad *today*." Don't wait until next Sunday in church. Say it tomorrow morning! Don't wait until next Tuesday or Wednesday, but say it today. Say, "This is the day God has made. I will rejoice and be glad in it."

When you and I choose to say this positive affirmation every day of the week, little by little, inch by inch, it begins to make a difference. Even when you do not feel like saying it, it will make a difference. You may not notice it tomorrow or the next day, but you'll wake up maybe a week or two, or maybe two months, from now and without any question you will see a positive difference in your life. It's what we call the daffodil principle.

I was told about a daffodil garden nearby in the mountains above Arrowhead Springs, California. Supposedly there are five acres of blooming daffodils. Can you imagine how large that garden is? It's supposed to be absolutely spectacular, like an ocean of bright yellow moving in the wind. And on the porch of a small house there hangs a sign that reads, "Answers to the questions I know you are asking." The next words on that sign read:

1. 50,000 bulbs
2. One at a time by one woman
3. Began in 1958

What is the daffodil principle? When one woman did one thing fifty-thousand times she changed a barren landscape into a waving sea of gold.

I don't know how many times you will need to quote the affirmation from Psalm 118:24—"This is the day the LORD has made; let us rejoice and be glad in it"—before the landscape of your life begins to change. But I do know it will.

Honor your present! Slow down and live in the moment of today, absorbing every nuance of what God brings across your path.

Journeys Have a Future

I once read about a retired lawyer in Arles, France, who very much wanted to rent a particular apartment when its current resident, a 90-year-old woman, died. In fact, he agreed to pay her an annuity of $500 a month for the right to inherit her lease upon her death. Time was on his side, he figured, assuming she had only a short time left to live. Thirty years later, in 1995, the woman was alive and well at 120 years of age—certified as the oldest living person at that time—and the lawyer was $180,000 poorer.

That story reminds me of another one in the Bible, found in James 4:13–17. In a parable of sorts, James reproves those who boast about what they are going to do "today or tomorrow"—like "go to this or that city, spend a year there, carry on business and make money." He says we don't know what's going to happen tomorrow, much less a year from now. Instead, he writes, here's what we should say: "If it is the Lord's will, we will live and do this or that."

The bottom line is you and I know nothing of the future—nothing! As quickly as the morning mist vanishes, James says, things can change. For that reason we are to hold the future lightly. For instance, if God has something He wants you to do for Him three years from now, He reserves the right to change what you do for the next two years to get you ready. That means whatever you were planning to do over the next two years may be off the table.

God sees everything—past, present, and future—at once. We see life only as a progression of events. Or, as our British friends like to define history, "One bloody thing after another!" God, therefore, sees your future with as much clarity as your present. For that reason, allow God's knowledge of your future to define who you are becoming.

A story I have heard often has become one of my favorites. I call it "The Story of Life" because it explains how God works in our lives.

The story takes place in China and concerns an old man who lives in the mountains with only two possessions—his son and his horse. One day the man's horse escaped from his corral and ran away, leaving the man with no way to plow his field. When his neighbors heard of his plight they gathered around, lamenting the old man's bad luck. "How do you know it's bad luck?" he asked them. They shrugged their shoulders and returned to their homes.

Then one day the man's horse suddenly appeared leading six other wild mares into the corral. The man's son quickly closed the gate and they rejoiced in their good fortune at now having seven horses instead of none.

Again the man's neighbors appeared, but this time they rejoiced: "Oh, what good luck you have had!" But the man said to them, "How do you know it's good luck?" His neighbors shrugged their shoulders and went home.

Not long after, the man's son was trying to tame the wild horses in the corral when he broke his leg, leaving him a cripple. When the neighbors heard about this, they came to visit the man, bemoaning his bad luck at having lost the help of his son. "How do you know this is bad luck?" the old man asked.

Soon after this event a warlord came through the mountains pressing every able-bodied man into his service as a soldier. The old man's son was passed over because he was crippled and could not march or fight. When his neighbors, whose sons had all been taken away, came to his house they exclaimed, "What good luck that your son was not taken!" And you know what the old man said.

That is the end of the telling of the story but not the end of the story itself, for it goes on and on indefinitely with the same cycle. The story is a picture of life—things happen to us but we do not know at the moment how to interpret them. They seem good or bad at the moment, but who knows what greater purpose may be at work?

The life of faith receives whatever comes and waits upon God to reveal its purpose. That is the Christian's hope according to Romans 8:28.

Honor your future! Live with an open hand, into and out of which God can give and take that which He knows your future will require.

Journeys Reveal Who We Are

I have just employed a good number of words to say we can be defined by our journey (past, present, and future), and now I'm about to say somewhat the opposite: our journey does not shape us as much as it reveals who we are so we might shape ourselves with God's help.

Take the Life-Journey of one of my favorite biblical characters, Joseph. By any measure of reality, Joseph underwent enough traumatic and disappointing events in his life to be excused, or at least understood, had he become a bitter person. For example, at the age of seventeen he was sold into slavery by his own brothers. When an Egyptian official purchased Joseph he was falsely accused of attempted rape by the official's wife and thrown into prison. There he was double-crossed by a fellow prisoner whom he helped to get released. (Read Joseph's story in Genesis 37–50.)

Through these events the real Joseph was revealed: a man who trusted wholly in the providence of God. He never got angry or bitter. Instead, he kept trusting in God and being blessed by Him, eventually realizing why God allowed every difficult event in his life: to put him in a position to save the Hebrew race (the family of Jacob) from starvation in Canaan.

Your journey has revealed you to be a certain kind of person today. Are you happy with what has been revealed? Not happy? God uses our journey to show us who we are in light of His goal for our lives—Christlikeness. Every time an event, encounter, or experience reveals something about who you are, embrace it and learn from it.

How do we strengthen our spirits to soar like an eagle? The only way is to fly into the wind, something that takes incredible strength. We would much rather do the easier thing—flying with the wind.

It's also a lot easier to float downstream than to swim upstream. The only problem is if you're floating downstream you always end up in the lowest possible spot since water always seeks the lowest level.

But anyone who has ever watched an eagle, or one of California's giant condors soar, knows what birds have learned: flying into the wind actually takes you higher. It's why airplanes take off into the wind—the air beneath their wings gives them lift they wouldn't otherwise have. Here in Southern California we have what are known as our "Santa Ana winds." They are so strong airplanes will change their direction whenever possible to fly directly into them to get the extra lift.

If we could learn this lesson we would likewise fly higher in our lives. If we would learn not to avoid the strong winds that blow but to face them head on, we would gain strength and elevation we would otherwise never experience. Jesus released a strong headwind when He said, "If anyone would come after me, he must deny himself and take up his cross and follow me" (Matt. 16:24).

If we do that, we will swim upstream, not float downstream. We will fly against the wind of this world, not with it. We will take the narrow road, not the wide one. But we will also find ourselves stronger, higher, and more focused than ever before.

Honor who you are! Don't run from or boast of what you discover about yourself. Instead, thank God for the insight and ask Him to use it to mold you into the image of Jesus.

Journeys Teach Us Not to Travel Alone

Are you familiar with the Rorschach Inkblot Test? That's the one where a series of ten cards with randomly shaped inkblots are shown to a patient to determine emotional and psychological characteristics. The client then describes what he sees in the shapes and colors—what they mean to him. The person administering the test is looking for what that individual alone sees. Because every person looks at life differently, every person's response to the ten cards will be different.

All of us have certain trips we make in the vicinity of where we live in which we are sometimes alone and other times in the company of our spouse, children, or a friend. I know that if I drive down the PCH—the Pacific Coast Highway in Orange County, California—with my wife I will see things I would not see if driving alone. Actually, I don't see the different things at all. *She* sees them and draws my attention to them: "Isn't that interesting? . . . Look over there . . . Is that new? . . . What happened to . . .?" I find that trips taken with other people are far more educational and edifying than trips taken alone.

I hope you are not journeying through life alone (regardless your marital state). To look at life through only one set of eyes is to limit life to only what you can see. Eventually, you believe what you see is what the world contains. Could anything be more egocentric—or more wrong? And how much better to travel with God who sees everything there is to see and is more than willing to show you. Even if you are traveling alone in this life, you aren't really alone—God *is* with you.

As I travel through our community and country meeting people, or when I'm asked to autograph one of my books, I use the sentence, "God is blessing you." Not "*May* God bless you" but "God *is* blessing you." You immediately see the difference, I'm sure. "May" implies God might, under some circumstance, decide to bless you in the future. But I believe God is blessing each of us right now. Like fish always surrounded by water, or humans in an atmosphere of oxygen, we are constantly enveloped by God's blessings—realize it, appreciate it, or not!

God began blessing you when you were born. That first gasp of air that filled your lungs was a gift from Him. Who else makes human life possible but God? And His blessing has continued from that moment to this. The realization of God's continual, present-tense blessing is a reason for living a continual, present-tense life of gratitude.

As a young man I visited the home of Corrie ten Boom where she lived in her latter years, not far from us in Southern California. Corrie was the marvelous Dutch Christian whose family hid Jews and others being pursued by the Nazis all over Europe. Corrie ended up in a German concentration camp herself from which she was eventually released.

Once when visiting in her home, she pulled from her pocket a blade of grass and told us the significance of it. "There was a point in my life in the concentration camp," she said, "when I didn't feel like I could go on another day. I woke up one day and I said, 'God, where are You? Are You alive or are You dead?'" All day she wrestled with the existence of God. When she went to sleep that night she was filled with anger toward God about the evil and horrors of the concentration camp.

When she awoke the next morning a beam of light was shining down through a tiny crack in the ceiling. She followed the stream of light and saw it was shining on a blade of grass in the corner of her cell that hadn't been there the day before—at least she never noticed it before. When she saw that tiny sign of life she knew God was there with her; that He had not forgotten her. Corrie was the only one of her family to survive the Nazi persecutions and one of the few who lived to tell of her experiences. In the deepest, darkest struggles of mankind and in the most hellish of circumstances, God is there. When we put on our glasses of gratitude we will begin to see the blessings of God surrounding us every day. We will never doubt He is with us, come what may.

Honor your fellow travelers! You will be shaped by iron sharpening iron (see Prov. 27:17) in a way you cannot be when traveling alone.

Journeys Keep Us Focused

The happiest, most fruitful people I know are those who can define their life focus with the most clarity. I've said God has a focus and a purpose for you—to become like His Son, Jesus Christ. But you have to have a focus as well—something you get up to accomplish each day *in the process of which God works out His purpose.*

It's not enough for us to rise in the morning and say, "I'm going to become more like Jesus." That's God's work. We have to have a focus that keeps us moving ahead on our Life-Journey. It is in pursuit of that journey where God accomplishes His work in us. Both those purposes—human and divine—are found in the apostle Paul's life. On the one hand his purpose was "to know Christ and the power of his resurrection" (Phil. 3:10). But on the other hand his purpose was "to carry [Christ's] name before the Gentiles and their kings and before the people of Israel" (Acts 9:15). As Paul stayed focused on his human, earthly purpose, God accomplished His divine purpose in him. And the more God conformed Paul to the image of Christ, the more effective he was in his human purpose.

It works the same for us. Our journey keeps us focused—it's a cycle feeding itself as we walk through life. But focus takes attention, energy, desire, and commitment. It is not something that happens apart from our participation. Rather it happens as we respond to what God is doing in us.

When I was ordained into the Christian ministry, my father gave me a special medallion. It was a beautiful gold piece about the size of a quarter with three Scripture references engraved on one side: Luke 9:62 ("Jesus replied, 'No one who puts his hand to the plow and looks back is fit for service in the kingdom of God.'"); Philippians 1:6 ("Being confident of this, that he who began a good work in you will carry it on to completion until the day of Christ Jesus"); and Revelation 2:10 ("Do not be afraid of what you are about to suffer. I tell you, the devil will put some of you in prison to test you, and you will suffer persecution for ten days. Be faithful, even to the point of death, and I will give you the crown of life.").

On the other side of the medallion was this inscription: "To my son, Reverend Robert A. Schuller, on your ordination into the Christian ministry. From your father, Reverend Robert H. Schuller, September 21, 1980."

I wore that medallion on a chain around my neck for eight years until a fateful day when my family was on vacation in Hawaii. I was sitting in a pool of water on the beach, playing with my two-year-old daughter. She climbed up onto my shoulders and, losing her balance, her hand caught the chain around my neck and the clasp broke. The chain and medallion both landed in the pool of sandy water.

Feeling frantically in the sand with my fingers, I felt the chain. But when I pulled it up the medallion fell off, back into the pool. For hours I searched for it, but to no avail. I even rushed to a store and bought a metal detector, but it didn't help. We left Hawaii and returned home, me without one of my most precious possessions.

Though I didn't have the medallion itself I never forgot the verses my father engraved on it. Those words, and the blessing from God and from him they represented, have served as guiding lights in my ministry. And I never gave up hope that somehow the medallion itself would find its way back to me. It took several years, but it happened. A person who happened to know who I was found the medallion in the sand on that beach in Hawaii and returned it to me.

It was another reminder to me that God's work is never done; that we ought never give up hope. Journeys need focus, and our focus has to remain on God. We never know what He is going to do for us, in us, and through us.

Honor your journey! Every step, every insight, every correction—believe God is walking and working with you, using your journey to define who you are becoming.

We are not accidents;
we were created for a
purpose. God, by His
Providence, oversees the
journey we are on.

Your Shoes Were Made for Walking

You intended to harm me, but God intended it for good to accomplish what is now being done, the saving of many lives.

—Genesis 50:20

The middle of five children, Tony always felt like the odd man out. His two older brothers made a pair, as did his two younger sisters. Stuck in the middle, he seemed determined to find his niche outside his family. Their move to a new town when he was in eighth grade didn't help matters, and he found friends he could well have done without. But they represented acceptance, so he fell in with them.

In high school, smoking led to marijuana that led to stealing to pay for drugs. He eventually dropped out of high school and supported himself dealing drugs on the street. He made lots of money, bought fancy cars, and became a player in the local drug scene. But run-ins with the law, car wrecks, full-fledged addiction to heroin and other hard drugs, several life-threatening overdoses, fathering a child, jail time, and unsuccessful rehabs led to several failed suicide attempts—veiled cries for help.

After more than a decade of this lifestyle—and wearing out the patience and forgiveness of his family many times over—Tony responded to a spark of faith that seemed still to glow somewhere deep inside. He learned about Jesus as a child, asked Him into his heart, and learned to pray—it was a natural part of his family's life as he grew up. But somewhere along the way the flame shrunk to a tiny ember, hidden behind the now-cold coals of childhood belief.

On his own he sought out a church reaching out to twenty-somethings in the uptown district of his metropolitan city. He began playing cards with guys he met at church—guys he knew wouldn't offer him things that could hurt him—in an attempt to lose his old crowd. He got to know the pastors—not much older than he was—and accepted an invitation to meet one of them for coffee.

The young pastor listened for a couple of hours, seemingly unsurprised as one sad chapter led to another in Tony's life story. He was one of the few people Tony ever talked to who hadn't shaken his head in disbelief at how a middle-class kid from the suburbs could have made so many bad choices for so long.

"I guess I'm at the point now that I can't see a real purpose for my life," Tony said, summing up. "I've hurt myself and so many other people in so many ways. I have no formal education. The only skills I have are either illegal or entry-level. I've got medical problems related to my past and I'm almost thirty years old. I've made such a mess out of the first third of my life that it's a little hard for me to see the purpose in trying to start over. Not to mention how God must look at my life after all the things I've done. Do you know what I mean?"

"I think I do," Randy said. "In fact, I know I do. Let me save us some time here by putting it this way: Had we tape-recorded the story you just told me, we could play it back and insert my name for yours and it would be pretty close to being my life story—up until about five years ago. That's why nothing you said to me was a surprise. I've done all your stuff, plus some things you didn't mention. And there was a point where I wondered what the purpose was, just like you."

Tony's eyes had gotten moist and his face flush listening to the pastor talk, so Randy picked up the thread and continued.

"But here's what I've discovered about failure, God, and my purpose in life. My purpose in life today—at this moment, in this coffee shop—is to identify with your purposelessness, because I've been there. I don't think God led me to sin and fail like I did so I could encourage you today. But once I chose to do those things, it didn't mean my life had no purpose. It *meant God had a purpose for me that would incorporate today everything in my life up through yesterday. In fact, my purpose in life tomorrow is going to incorporate what I learn from you in our conversation today.*

"I'm not smart enough to figure out how God works out the details—how He incorporates my failures into His purpose. All I know is my life does have purpose now that I've begun to see my failures are not bigger than His plans. I wish I hadn't messed up so much of my life. But having done that, my purpose in life today is to tell you that God loves me—and you—today in spite of who and what we might have been yesterday."

L ATE IN LIFE, JOHN NEWTON often referred to himself as "the old African blasphemer"—because that's what he was.

John's mother was a pious Christian who tried to raise her son biblically in eighteenth-century England. But she died when he was just seven years old and his upbringing became the responsibility of his sea-faring father and his stepmother, neither of whom continued his spiritual training. Traveling on sea voyages with his father put saltwater in his veins, and he went on to become a captain himself.

But it was John Newton's extracurricular life at which history stands amazed. He invested himself in every kind of debauchery and blasphemy life on ships and the docks offered. And he delighted in mocking those who attempted to live otherwise, doing his best to lead them down the same path. He would make occasional attempts at reforming his character, harkening back to the childhood teachings of his mother. But invariably he ended up in a lifestyle that seemed to have little value or purpose.

The "African" part of John's blasphemous life happened when he found himself involved in the African slave trade while still a young man. On a voyage from Africa to England his ship was almost lost in a violent storm. So terrified was he that he threw himself upon the mercy of God to save him, pouring over the pages of the Bible while the ship was tossed around the North Atlantic.

As a result of this experience, which John would later mark as a definite conversion point, his moral life changed. He gave up the wanton and blasphemous life he had been living, though he did not exit the slave trade until several years later. It was during another trip to Africa that he was forced to admit the shallow depth of his spiritual life, calling out to God yet again for mercy. Back in England, John Newton began to come under the influence of evangelical preaching from the likes of George Whitefield and John and Charles Wesley. He soon left the slave trade and the seafaring life altogether.

Could we have interviewed John Newton at various points during his late teens—for example, when he was being beaten and treated like a dog, forced to eat off the floor, by the cruel wife of a trader in Africa who purchased Newton as a servant—and asked him, "John, what is the purpose of your life?" he would have been hard-pressed to answer very positively. His was a debauched and morally vacuous life, and he was being given by life what he seemingly deserved—a purposeless life without value or direction.

But if we were to fast-forward to the latter half of the eighteenth century we would find a John Newton whose life was brimming with purpose. He taught himself Hebrew, Greek, Syriac, and theology in his spare time and was ordained, after many years of apprenticing and applying, into the priesthood of the Anglican church in England. His sermons and counsel were so valued, people came from great distances to hear him preach and seek his advice. It was his counsel to William Wilberforce, member of Parliament, that convinced the young abolitionist to remain in Parliament and fight for the abolition of the slave trade altogether, advice which Wilberforce took and spent the next five decades implementing.

With the poet, William Cowper, Newton published *Olney Hymns* in 1779, a book of some of the most famous hymns in the history of the church. Indeed, John Newton's hymn "Amazing Grace" may be the most widely known and loved song in history, by Christians and non-Christians alike. He also wrote his own autobiographical account of "amazing grace" along with other theological works.

Would anyone deny that John Newton's life had great purpose once he left the slave trade, committed himself to Christ, and became a pastor, hymn writer, counselor to leaders, and theologian? Where did John Newton cross the line from purposeless living to purposeful living? And where was God in the process? Did God have a purpose for John Newton's life only after he left the sea and took to the pulpit? Or was God involved in "the old African blasphemer's" life from the start?

A good way to think about these questions using John Newton as an example is to consider this: How would Newton the hymn writer have been able to pen these lines—

Amazing grace! How sweet the sound,
That saved a wretch like me!
I once was lost but now am found,
Was blind but now I see.

without first having been Newton the blasphemer and slave trader? His ability to plumb the depths of the amazing grace of God was only possible because he first plumbed the depths of sin and degradation.

But this raises another question: was it God's purpose for John Newton to sin as a blasphemer and slave trader so he might later repent and proclaim the depths of God's grace and forgiveness? If so, does that not make Jesus' model prayer problematic—"And lead us not into temptation, but deliver us from the evil one" (Matt. 6:13)?

I have studied and thought about questions like this my whole Christian experience. And here is what I have concluded: The reason these deep questions about the purposes of God and the purpose of man remain fresh is because they are essentially unanswerable at the level of detail we would like. We have to live with a level of tension that we would prefer to do away with by having nice, neat theological and practical answers to all of our deepest questions about our lives.

But this we can do: We can prayerfully study and meditate upon God's revelation of Himself to us in Scripture and in His Son, Jesus Christ, and draw what conclusions we can, knowing that there are some "secret things [that] belong to the LORD our God" (Deut. 29:29). And with what God has revealed to us we can conclude that regardless of where we are in life, God has a purpose for us. But will we open our eyes to see and embrace it?

Whatever weaknesses you think exist in your own background that might keep God from using you—forget about them. God is more than happy to equip those who have used up all their own resources.

Here are five points to consider that will encourage you to believe, regardless of where you are today—whether prodigal or preacher—God has a purpose for your life.

Man: the Accident

There are many people today who believe man is an accident of nature. That is, generally they are evolutionists who do not believe that a God with a purpose created the world in which we live. They believe man is the long-term result of bits and pieces of primordial soup bumping into one another long enough to—shazaaam!—cause life to spontaneously emerge.

While there are many people who believe that today, I wonder how many of them have considered the ultimate implications of such belief when it comes to purpose in life? It was, I believe, in the writings of the late theologian Francis Schaeffer where I was first caused to consider the contradictions of such a position. He made the point it's fine to take an existentialist position—that we live only for today; there are no absolutes; our existence is unexplainable; man has no real purpose—if you're willing to live with the consequences. Schaeffer suggested that as soon as a thief steals such a person's wallet, a purposeless worldview becomes less attractive. It's fine to live in a purposeless world until someone else's behavior makes your own life uncomfortable. Suddenly, one innately senses a need to bring purpose and order to the chaos causing one's unhappy state.

If man is nothing but an accident of evolution, the implications for purpose are obvious: there can be no ultimate purpose. Of course, individuals can think up their own purpose and seek to fulfill it. But what happens if some person turns out to be a murderous tyrant who believes his purpose is to subjugate others? At that point groups of people might come together and decide their collective purpose is to resist and negate the purpose of the tyrant. And on and on. Life becomes nothing more than a pinball game where individuals and their self-conceived purposes compete with one another for meaning and supremacy.

The English novelist George Eliot wrote in *Daniel Deronda*, "What makes life dreary is the want of motive." And accidents cannot have motives. *If you believe you are an evolutionary accident, you will only frustrate yourself searching for a purpose in life.* But if you are not an accident, as the Bible tells us, the opposite is true: your life does have a motive, a purpose.

A young boy came home from Sunday school one day and said, "Dad, I know everything there is to know about the Bible."

"Really, son?"

"Oh yes," the boy continued, "I went to Sunday school today and I learned everything I need to know."

"And what is that?"

"The Bible is basic information before leaving earth," the boy replied. "B-I-B-L-E. Basic Information Before Leaving Earth."

There is obviously more to know. But that acronym at least suggests the fact that man is no accident—God has a plan for taking people from earth to heaven to live with Him forever.

Man: the Plan

So the first question in need of answer is, how did I get here? The Bible has a clear answer for that question in a "micro" and a "macro" sense.

From the micro perspective the early chapters of Genesis say the world and everything in it was created intentionally (on purpose) by God. Man was fashioned from the dust of the earth and given life by the breath of God. The man's wife-counterpart was fashioned from one of his ribs. The couple was then given their first assignment (purpose) on earth: to tend the garden of God and to oversee the rest of God's creation.

Some Bible students choose to see more metaphor than fact in the micro view of the creation story while still agreeing wholeheartedly with the macro view: that mankind was created in the image of God for the purpose of being God's stewards over all creation. Mankind alone, being in the image of God, is unique on the earth from all the rest of the animal kingdom. While it's true the animal kingdom expresses intelligence and emotion in varying degrees, it is plainly obvious human beings are uniquely different, and therefore have a God-given purpose in the creation story.

To be honest, I have to recognize at this point a school of thought which stands midway between the evolution/accident view of man and the creation/purpose view: deism, which I mentioned briefly in chapter one. It recognizes God's existence and that God even created the earth and everything in it. But ever since creation, according to this view, God maintains no purpose for planet Earth or for mankind. Deism is just a theory—an idea. It has no more credibility than any other idea, whether reasonable or far-fetched, that might be invented to explain the existence of creation and mankind. It certainly can claim no biblical support. It could not be more evident that God has been intimately involved with man since creation. God has not abandoned man to seek his own way in the world.

Twice in the Psalms David expresses his confidence that God has a purpose for him:

"I cry out to God Most High, to God, who fulfills his purpose for me." (57:2)

"The LORD will fulfill his purpose for me; your love, O LORD, endures forever—do not abandon the works of your hands." (138:8)

David never hesitated to call on God when he was in trouble, because he believed God had purpose for his life and he didn't want his purpose to go unfulfilled. He wanted to be saved, rescued, delivered, put back on track, set on solid ground, given victory over his enemies—because He wanted to fulfill His purpose in life.

God created this world and everything in it—including you—for a purpose. That's the only conclusion I can draw. There is a plan and you are part of it.

Plans Have a Purpose

One of the most powerful examples of the confluence of God's plan and purpose is the story of Joseph in the Old Testament. I briefly mentioned Joseph in the last chapter, but let me fill in a few more details revealing how God's purposes were at work in his life.

When God established His covenant with Abraham, Joseph's great-grandfather (see Gen. 12:1–3; 15:1–19), He promised that Abraham would be the father of a great nation with innumerable descendants. By the time Abraham's grandson, Jacob, had a family, the number of Abraham's descendants (through the promised line of Abraham's son Isaac) reached around seventy: Jacob's twelve sons and one daughter and their spouses and children.

Jacob's favorite son was Joseph, and out of jealousy his brothers devised a plan to get rid of him. They sold him as a slave to a group of traders heading for Egypt and told their father his favorite son was killed by a wild animal. This experience, along with other situations in Egypt, no doubt gave Joseph plenty of reasons to question God's purpose for his life. Nonetheless, for the next twenty years Joseph's stature in Egypt was elevated until he became the second most powerful man in the nation—the right-hand man to Pharaoh himself.

During this same period, the fortunes of God's future chosen people were deteriorating rapidly. The same character qualities that led Jacob's eleven sons to sell the twelfth into slavery caused them to engage in other morally reprehensible acts, illustrated by the story of Judah in Genesis 38. The children of Jacob—the descendants of Abraham—were in danger of becoming morally and spiritually corrupt by involvement with their pagan neighbors.

To move his fledgling family to a place where they could grow in a secluded environment away from moral temptation, God sent a famine to Canaan and Egypt. But Joseph had prepared Egypt for the coming famine. Through a series of dramatic encounters with the brothers who sold him into slavery, Joseph sent for Jacob and all his family. They came to a land that despised shepherds and so were isolated in a corner of the kingdom where they grew into a nation of several million by the time of the Exodus.

God had a purpose for Joseph: go to Egypt and prepare a place for His chosen people to grow into a nation. Joseph caught a glimpse of God's purpose and plan and told his brothers, "You intended to harm me [by selling me into slavery], but God intended it for good to accomplish what is now being done, the saving of many lives" (Gen. 50:20).

Plans have a purpose. Because you are part of God's plan, you have a purpose as well.

Purposes Require Preparation

Genesis 50:20 is like the Old Testament version of one of the most well-known truths in the New Testament: "And we know that in all things God works for the good of those who love him, who have been called according to his purpose" (Rom. 8:28). Both these verses contain words spoken by men who understood that truth: Joseph and the apostle Paul. Paul is a prime example of how purposes often require preparation.

The first (approximately) thirty years of Paul's life were spent preparing for leadership in Judaism. His pedigree was spotless: "If anyone else thinks he has reasons to put confidence in the flesh, I have more: circumcised on the eighth day, of the people of Israel, of the tribe of Benjamin, a Hebrew of Hebrews; in regard to the law, a Pharisee; as for zeal, persecuting the church; as for legalistic righteousness, faultless" (Phil. 3:4–6). He was a student of Gamaliel, one of Israel's most respected rabbis (see Acts 22:3) and would have been considered first in his class, or *summa cum laude*, by today's standards of excellence (see Gal. 1:14). His knowledge of the Scriptures was no doubt encyclopedic—as evidenced by the way he seamlessly wove Scripture quotations into his epistles.

In light of Paul's zealous Jewish background, it would be hard to imagine a more shocking conversion to Christ than his. But Paul was saved for a particular purpose as expressed by Christ Himself: "This man is my chosen instrument to carry my name before the Gentiles and their kings and before the people of Israel" (Acts 9:15). Christ later told Paul, "I am sending you to [the Gentiles] to open their eyes and turn them from darkness to light" (Acts 26:17–18).

This was revolutionary news! The God of the Jews—the God of Abraham, Isaac, and Jacob—was about to begin inviting non-Jews (Gentiles) to come into the fold and be saved. Paul called this a "mystery," something concealed in the Old Testament but now to be revealed through him: "This mystery is that through the gospel the Gentiles are heirs together with Israel, members together of one body, and sharers together in the promise in Christ Jesus" (Eph. 3:6).

Now—if you were God, and that was your purpose, who would you choose to convey that message? Someone zealous, committed, intelligent, and tireless? Of course. But above all, someone with a thorough knowledge of the past (the Old Testament) upon which the present and future would be built. God chose an Old Testament scholar, a man unknowingly preparing for this purpose for thirty years, to reveal to Jews and non-Jews alike how all people were going to be brought together into one new body called the church of Jesus Christ.

Sometimes unique purposes require unique preparation. In fact, all purposes require some preparations. And God is able to use everything in your life so far toward the end of achieving His purpose for you.

Purpose and Paradigms

Here's how *The American Heritage Dictionary* defines a paradigm: "A set of assumptions, concepts, values, and practices that constitutes a way of viewing reality." And based on my experience, I believe many people, even many Christians who believe their Bibles, live their lives with a faulty paradigm—a non-biblical paradigm. Why? Because they don't believe God has a purpose for their lives. Or if He does, He has hidden it from them.

We often hear people say, "I'll believe it when I can see it!" But, as is often the case in the kingdom of God, the reverse is usually true: "I'll see it when I believe it." In other words, sometimes it takes a paradigm shift—a new way of looking at reality—before we can begin to see what God is doing in our lives. Jesus spoke of having "eyes to see" when teaching His disciples. Even they did not always comprehend God's purposes in Christ's life or their own. Gradually, they replaced their old paradigms with a new one. They replaced their old wineskins with new ones which could accommodate the new wine of Jesus' teaching (see Luke 5:37–38).

As I have already mentioned, David the psalmist had a paradigm that incorporated God's purpose for his life. Nowhere did he express that more completely than in Psalm 139:15–16: "My frame was not hidden from you when I was made in the secret place. When I was woven together in the depths of the earth, your eyes saw my unformed body. *All the days ordained for me were written in your book before one of them came to be*" (emphasis added).

The last line of that verse represents how David viewed his life—and how we ought to view ours: as ordained by God from beginning to end. *Finding and fulfilling one's purpose in life requires a paradigm shift—learning to view our lives from God's perspective instead of our own.*

I cannot tell you how every victory and every defeat in your past or present figures into God's purpose for your life. But I can tell you with certainty five things:

1. You are not an accident, adrift in a world without purpose.
2. You are part of God's creation plan, meaning your life has purpose.
3. God's purpose for your life will be achieved by a plan worked out over time.
4. Every day of your life adds to your ability to accomplish God's purpose for your life.
5. You may need to open your eyes of faith wider in order to see how God intends to accomplish His purpose for your life.

My encouragement to you is this:

First, believe God. Believe you are part of His purposeful creation.

Second, don't agonize over the past and future of your purpose in life. Believe God was in your past and will be in your future and *is* in your present.

Third, pray a prayer like this: "Lord, open the eyes of my heart. Help me see my life from Your loving perspective. Help me believe Romans 8:28—that You are using everything in my life to accomplish Your purpose for me."

Whether you know it or not (or even believe it or not) you are in some stage of God's unfolding purpose for your life. And there is no better place for you to be.

I love the story of the "fourth" wise man. Tradition says he left with the other three to follow the star in search of the newborn king of the Jews. But as they traveled this fourth wise man was continually being distracted by people they met along the way, people who needed various kinds of help. He would send the other three ahead and catch up within a day or two. But when the other three reached Bethlehem, the fourth wise man was nowhere to be found.

Finally, he arrived in Jerusalem—three days after the crucifixion of Jesus. He mourned and wept aloud, grieving over the fact the king He came to worship had already grown up and been put to death. He spent thirty years giving help to others in need and missed the one person he most wanted to see.

Suddenly, on that third day, Jesus was raised from the dead and appeared to the fourth wise man. When the wise man started to apologize for never arriving on time to worship Him at His birth, Jesus stopped him: "For I was hungry and you gave me something to eat, I was thirsty and you gave me something to drink, I was a stranger and you invited me in, I needed clothes and you clothed me, I was sick and you looked after me, I was in prison and you came to visit me" (Matt. 25:35–36).

Every person has a purpose and a destiny ordained by God. As you reach out and touch those He puts in your path you will be fulfilling part of your purpose, regardless of whatever else you are called to do. When you respond faithfully to the ministry God sets before you, there is no higher calling than to fulfill it.

God's goal is to conform
you to the image of
Jesus Christ and have you
dwell with Him for eternity.
Your life only makes sense
in light of that goal.

All Roads Lead to Home

And we know that in all things God works for the good of those who love him, who have been called according to his purpose. For those God foreknew he also predestined to be conformed to the likeness of his Son, that he might be the firstborn among many brothers.

—Romans 8:28–29

It was the summer before Jessica's senior year in high school, and she and her parents were deep into the college prep process. Specifically, they were trying to choose the colleges to which Jessie should apply. The problem was, like lots of rising high school seniors, Jessie had no idea what she wanted to "be" in life—what she wanted to do after she went to college.

In one of their informal discussions on the subject that summer, Jessie was stuck on this reverse line of reasoning: "If I don't know what I want to be or do, I don't know what to major in. And if I don't know what to major in, I don't know which college to go to. And if I don't know which college to go to, I don't know which colleges even to apply to."

"Well, I like your powers of logic and reasoning," Jessie's dad said, smiling. "Maybe you could major in that."

"Very funny, Dad. I'm serious. If I don't know where I'm going to end up, how am I supposed to know where to start?"

Sensing they had stumbled into a moment where Jessie was willing to keep the discussion going, Bob sat up a little straighter and glanced at Barb, his wife, to encourage her input. "Jessie, maybe we could look at this thing the opposite way," he began. "You're trying to figure out something you don't need to know for at least five years—that is, what kind of vocation or direction you want to take after college. That's asking a lot for someone your age. I mean, if you happened to have your heart set on something now, that would be fine. But it's not wrong, or a weakness, if you don't."

"I agree," Barb said. "Part of the college experience is for you to be exposed to lots of different areas of interest. Sometimes the journey is the most important part of the process; you discover the destination along the way."

"I didn't know it at the time," Bob continued, "but one of the best things that happened to me was going to a smaller liberal arts college. I didn't know what I wanted to do either when I enrolled. But in the process of taking courses in lots of different subjects, I gradually began to realize there were things I liked and things I didn't like. By my junior year I was taking more electives in electrical engineering and computer science. Because I was at a small college I was able to get to know my professors well and observe their lifestyle as professors and consultants to outside tech companies. And by the time I was a senior I knew I wanted to go on to graduate school in computer science and—voilà!—I ended up with a PhD—a certified computer geek. I went to work for a couple of companies and now have my own computer consulting business. But did I know that's where I'd end up the summer before my senior year in high school? No way!"

"Jessie, think of it this way," Barb said. "When you enter college, all the people in your class will have the same ten-year goal: be productive and happy doing something they enjoy. And I dare say the vast majority of those people will achieve that goal, including you. But just think of all the different paths people will take to reach that same goal. Some will get there by way of business, some by medicine, some by the military, some by being a housewife, some by owning their own companies, like Dad, and a million other paths. While the goal is the same for everyone, everyone gets there a different way. There's no book to read on how to do this. You just begin the journey and trust your path will become more and more clear with each step."

Jessie listened quietly to her parents and she knew they were waiting on her to respond. "Well, the idea of a small college appeals to me, and if you guys don't think you'd be wasting your money if I just start off taking gen-

eral courses, then I think I'd be willing to do that—and trust that I'll reach my goal at the right time."

"That's fine with us, Jess," Bob said. "God has a goal for your life. Your path to that goal will be unique—like no one else's. And remember—it's a journey, a path, a process. The first step is to begin. If you do that, God will be with you to show you what you need to know, when you need to know it."

A T ITS PEAK, THE ROMAN Empire stretched from England in the north, Spain in the west, North Africa in the south, and Palestine, Syria, and Asia Minor in the east. It was huge. And with typical military efficiency, what Rome conquered, Rome dominated and developed. In order to move people, armies, and commercial interests into newly conquered lands, Rome built roads. It is for that reason the saying emerged, somewhere during Rome's history, "All roads lead to Rome."

Rome had a goal and a purpose for everything she conquered: that they become Roman. But "Roman" in England looked different from "Roman" in Palestine. And that was fine. Because linking all the parts of that far-flung empire were the roads tying everything to Rome. It was not hard for Rome to move armies, laws, information, and culture into new possessions because they had the roads. And all roads led to Rome. There was the *Via Appia*, the *Via Fulvia*, the *Via Aurelia*, the *Via Flavia*, the *Via Flaminia*, and many others. So well were these roads constructed that many of them are still visible. And many of them have developed into modern transportation arteries throughout Europe. Towns developed along these roads are major cities today.

Are you familiar with the mile-marker signs on our modern freeways? They have their roots in the orderly system of Roman roads. In 20 B.C., a *miliarium aureum*—the golden milestone—was set up in Rome near the temple of Saturn. All roads leading out of Rome, and mile markers along the way, were said to be measured from that point. Emperor Constantine called it the *umbilicus Romae*—the navel of Rome. On it were listed all the major cities in the empire and the distances to them.

The thousands of milestones set up along Roman roads were impressive. They were round stone columns, twenty inches in diameter, set on a rectangular base buried in the ground. The markers were several feet high and weighed a couple tons—and were not easily moved. On the marker was written the number of the mile from its beginning point in Rome and other information about the road and its builders.

Wherever you traveled in the Roman empire, as long as you were on a Roman road you knew where you were. You knew how far you were from the heart of the empire and how to get there if need be. Every fifteen to eighteen miles or so Roman *mansiones* (staying places) were built—villas dedicated to the refreshment of official Roman travelers. In time, hostel-like accommodations sprung up along the way for non-official travelers.

If you were a Roman citizen traveling on a Roman road, your needs were met. If you set out from what is today England, France, Turkey, Egypt, Israel, or the Balkans, and wanted to reach Rome, it was possible. You were like a red blood cell in the human body. Eventually you would make it to the heart of the system. There was great security in knowing all roads led to Rome.

All Roads Lead to Home

There is a similar security, for the believer in Jesus Christ, in knowing all roads lead to home. While we normally think of home as heaven—and it certainly is our ultimate, eternal destiny—there's another way to think of home in terms of your personal life. Remember what I said the purpose was for all the lands Rome conquered and populated? It was to make them Roman. In a similar sense, God has one central purpose for the life of every follower of Jesus: to make them like Christ.

In essence, that's what the word *Christian* means: little Christ, or Christ-one. The Bible couldn't be more clear about this ultimate purpose God has for you and for me. One of the verses I quoted at the beginning of this chapter says it plainly: "For those God foreknew he also predestined to be conformed to the likeness of his Son, that [Jesus] might be the firstborn among many brothers" (Rom. 8:29). In the next verse, Paul relates this purpose as pretty much a done deal: "And those [God] predestined, he also called; those he called, he also justified; those he justified, he also glorified."

If you've been called into a relationship with Christ, you've also been justified. That means you've been declared righteous (sinless) in God's sight because Christ paid the penalty for your sins. And if you've been justified (made sinless like Christ), then you've also been glorified. Paul is talking about something that will happen in the future when we are resurrected to begin a glorious eternal life in heaven—but he's talking about it in the past tense, as if it has already happened. And in God's sight, it has. It's a done deal. In other words, God views you *now* as you someday *will be:* like Christ in all His glory!

What this means to you as a Christian is, whoever you are and wherever you are, all roads lead to home—to Christlikeness. God is going to accomplish His ultimate purpose for you. You are going to become one of Jesus' many brothers and sisters (read the last phrase of verse 29 again). Just like a Roman citizen always felt tied to Rome when he or she was traveling on a Roman road, so you ought to feel securely tied to God—to His purpose of conforming you to Christ—whoever and wherever you are.

But a disconnect occurs in our security level at times. Things happen in our lives—the equivalent of a Roman citizen taking a wrong turn and finding himself on a road with no mile markers—that give us a sense of being lost. We lose sight of God's good and ultimate purpose in our lives because of circumstances we go through. We feel guilty or shameful because of things we do. We feel angry, hurt, or resentful because of things done to us. Or we feel dazed, confused, or overwhelmed with the enormity of life and its challenges.

Whatever the case or cause, we know this: we don't feel very Christlike. We think to ourselves, *Jesus wouldn't feel ashamed. Jesus wouldn't be resentful. Jesus wouldn't be confused.* When our humanity overshadows our glory like a big, black cloud, it's easy to lose sight of God's ultimate purpose in our lives. It's easy to question whether we will ever reach God's goal in this life of becoming conformed to Christ. Or whether we'll just struggle in our humanity until we die and only then experience the reality of transformation.

The apostle Paul knew you and I wouldn't be the only people ever to have those doubts and concerns. That's why he wrote in Philippians 1:6,

"There has never been the slightest doubt in my mind that the God who started this great work in you would keep at it and bring it to a flourishing finish on the very day Christ Jesus appears" (The Message). And he wrote in 1 Thessalonians, "The One who called you is completely dependable. If he said it, he'll do it!" (5:23 The Message).

But there's another reason you can know all God's roads in your life lead to home. And it's sitting in the verse just before Romans 8:29. Next to John 3:16, Romans 8:28 may be the most well-known—or at least the most clung-to—verse in the New Testament: "And we know that in all things God works for the good of those who love him, who have been called according to his purpose." Whether we stub our toe or experience an unexpected disaster or loss, we are quick to quote Romans 8:28.

But if we take this great promise in the context in which Paul is writing, it is obvious he is addressing God's purpose (end of v. 28) to conform us to the image of Christ (v. 29). In other words, all the things that happen in our lives that have the potential to destroy our security in God and make us feel utterly lost, are the things God uses "for the good of those who love him" in order to conform us "to the likeness of his Son."

Romans 8:28 is not just a promise to make good people feel better when bad things happen. It's not the Christian version of *que será, será* ("whatever will be, will be") or *así es la vida* ("such is life"). It is not a Christian version of fatalism or a good luck charm or a way to promote a stiff upper lip when things aren't going well. Sadly, that's how many think of Romans 8:28.

Instead, Romans 8:28 is a promise from God that says, if you love Him, He is going to use everything that happens in your life to bring about His ultimate purpose of transforming you into the image of Jesus Christ. That's a whole lot different, and a whole lot better, than, "Hey— keep looking up! Things'll work out for the best!" Because of Romans 8:28–29, all roads lead to home for you.

Kingdom Roads

Rome had her roads taking her citizens where they needed to go, and the kingdom of God has its roads as well. In the process of our transformation into the image of Jesus Christ every Christian will travel all these roads. The first three are the main arteries we travel on; the second three are the return ramps by which we continue our transformation when we find we've made a wrong turn.

First is the road of *faith*.

As I work on this book I am basking in the afterglow of another glorious Christmas season. If ever there is a time when faith and hope are embraced by the church, and even by the non-Christian world, it has to be Christmas. We see a simple, yet intense, version of hope as we watch little kids shake their presents to try and tell if they are getting what they are hoping for. (And we bigger kids do the same thing when we're sure no one is looking.)

But that's the world's version of hope—a desire and longing with no basis in fact, no certainty in promise.

For the Christian, we travel through life with a different kind of faith, the kind described in Hebrews 11:1: "Now faith is being sure of what we hope for and certain of what we do not see." Being sure and certain is different from hoping without any kind of assurance of what will happen.

When we are traveling toward home, walking in what we believe is God's purpose for our lives, things can happen to destroy our confidence. And that is where faith steps in. The moment we get off the road of faith we are no longer headed for home. When we're traveling in the dark it takes faith—certainty, assuredness—to keep walking, believing God is working out His purpose.

How is your faith right now? Are you certain God is at work to transform you into the image of Jesus?

Next is the road of *grace*.

There have been many times when I've shared the gospel of salvation with someone in a conversational setting and he or she has asked, "Saved from what?" It's a fair question. And the ultimate answer, according to Scripture, is we are saved from being lost—separated from God—for eternity.

But God's road of grace is much wider than that one answer. There are lots of things God saves us *from* and even things He saves us *for*. Look at Ephesians 2:8, 10: "For it is by grace you have been saved, through faith. . . . For we are God's workmanship, created in Christ Jesus to do good works, which God prepared in advance for us to do."

The Christian's entire life is lived by grace—by God's power instead of our own. God, by His grace, saves us *from* hopelessness, *from* despair, *from* self-centeredness, *from* sin, and *from* purposelessness. And He saves us *for* the good things He has called us to accomplish. Just as God sent Christ into the world for a purpose, so He sends us into the world with a purpose as well. Every step of our journey toward home is taken by grace. The road of God's grace is no single-lane dirt road. It is a multilane superhighway on which we travel with freedom and happiness on our way home.

Are you trying to accomplish your purpose in life in your own strength? Or are you walking by God's grace—in His strength?

The third road is the road of *love*.

Every year at Christmas we invite children from all over the surrounding area to come to the Crystal Cathedral to view a pageant we call "The Glory of Christmas." Literally thousands of children visit our campus to view the biblical story of Christmas. This past Christmas, one of our staff members heard a little boy say to his friend, "Where's all the Christmas stuff?" Because the little boy hadn't seen Santa Claus he didn't think he'd seen anything having to do with Christmas.

That's exactly why we invite children to view "The Glory of Christmas"; to give them some understanding of what Christmas really means. So many children, and adults as well, can go through the Christmas season—indeed, go through all their lives—and know nothing of the love of God as manifested in the birth of the Christ child.

And if that is not heartbreaking enough, there are many Christians who seek to find purpose in life without resting in the love God has for them. They work and agonize, forgetting that our road through life is on the road of God's love. John 3:16 says God loved us so much He gave us His best gift—His Son, Jesus. And Romans 8:32 says that if God didn't hold back His best, won't He give us, with Jesus, everything else we need? Of course He will!

Would you say to yourself right now, "God loves me!"? And would you remind yourself of that fact whenever you feel unloved?

Faith, grace, and love are three of God's widest roads on which we walk toward Christlikeness. Becoming like Jesus is not something we do on our own. In fact, it's something we *can't* do on our own. The only way we can achieve the ultimate purpose of God in our lives is to allow Christ to live in and through us as Paul says in Galatians 2:20: "I have been crucified with Christ and I no longer live, but Christ lives in me [there's the road of grace]. The life I live in the body, I live by faith [there's the road of faith] in the Son of God, who loved me [there's the road of love] and gave himself for me."

If you are going to realize God's purpose of transformation into the image of Christ in your life, it will only be as you walk by faith and in God's love and grace.

But what about the inevitable times when we don't? Here's a mundane example that will make my point: Being a great fan of college football, I boldly announced during the 2006 season that there was no way UCLA would beat USC. I even said hell would freeze over first! Between these two arch-rival powerhouses, USC held the edge in total wins in the schools' first seventy-six years of competition. But UCLA held the record for the longest consecutive-winning streak—eight years from 1991 to 1998. In 2006 USC had the opportunity to tie that record after winning seven games from 1999 through 2005. So I thought I was on pretty good ground when I publicly (make that arrogantly) declared USC would trounce UCLA.

But if you keep up with college football you know I was eating a huge dish of humble pie on the night of December 2, 2006, after UCLA beat USC 13 to 9.

Fortunately, there was little damaged in that incident except my pride and my reputation for humility and wisdom (actually, the lack of it). But what if something far more critical had been at stake? What if, instead of a football game, I said something that wasn't true, or that hurt another person, or damaged another's reputation? Or what if I engaged in behavior completely un-Christlike?

When those things happen (note: not *if* they happen, but *when* they happen), there are three on-ramps God provides us to get back on His kingdom roads: confession, forgiveness, and repentance. I'll mention these briefly, not because they are unimportant but because this is a reminder, not an introduction.

The road of *confession*.

The Greek word for confession is *homologeo,* and it means to say (*logeo*) the same (*homo*) as. When we confess our un-Christlike attitudes and actions, we're saying the same thing God says about them. And it's not confession until we do. If we hem and haw and rationalize and blame, we're not confessing. Until our perception of our life is the same as God's, we're not confessing.

God invites us to confess (1 John 1:9). To turn down that invitation is to live life off God's roads to home.

The road of *forgiveness*.

Forgiveness is the flip side of the confession coin; it's what follows when we agree with God about our actions and attitudes.

David, the king of Israel, lived almost a year of life with the double sins of adultery and accomplice to murder on his conscience. And he was miserable. When God called him to account (see 2 Sam. 11–12) David got right: "I said, 'I will confess my transgressions to the LORD'—and you forgave the guilt of my sin" (Ps. 32:5).

There are no one-sided coins in God's kingdom. You don't get the forgiveness side without the confession side. But you do get forgiveness when you confess. It's the only way to get back on the road to home.

The road of *repentance*.

The Greek verb for repentance (*metanoeo*) literally means "to change one's mind or purpose." It's the second of those two words—purpose—that is important for us in this discussion: *We will never realize God's purpose for our lives by living according to our own actions and attitudes.* When we repent of our sins we are saying to God, "I got off Your road, Lord, trying to accomplish my own purposes in life. I repent. I choose Your purpose for my life instead of mine. I get back on Your roads of faith, grace, and love and I get off the roads of selfish ambition, fear, and pride. I would rather be like Jesus than be like me."

In the Roman empire, all roads led to Rome. But in the kingdom of God, all roads lead to home—and home is Jesus and becoming like Him. If you are not sure at this point in your life of any other of God's purposes for you, you can be sure of this: God's ultimate purpose for you is to conform you into the image of Jesus. If you are called according to

His purpose (see Rom. 8:28), be certain and sure that each day you are becoming more like Him.

And, by the way, don't be surprised at the methods God uses to accomplish that goal in your life. I didn't realize at the time that looking at the front page of the newspaper one day was the beginning of God's way to achieve His purposes in and through my life.

On the front page of the *Orange County Register* was a picture of a poor Mexican fisherman sitting atop a pile of rubble that used to be his home. His house, and most of those in his coastal village, La Carbonera, was destroyed by a hurricane. I was sitting in my comfortable office on that Monday morning looking at that picture thinking, *Gee, what a terrible thing. Poor guy.*

Then my wife, Donna, stopped by my office. I showed her the picture and told her how sorry I felt for the Mexican fisherman—no insurance on his home, no way to rebuild, nowhere to live. I think I concluded my words with, "Too bad there's no one to help him."

Donna looked at me and said, "Well, you could help him."

"Me?"

"Yes. You could do something about his plight if you wanted to." (Guys, don't you just hate it when God uses wives this way?)

The next day I was on a Missionary Aviation Fellowship airplane headed for La Carbonera, Mexico, to help this fisherman rebuild his home. But when I got there I learned it wasn't that easy. The official in charge of the area said, "You can't build one house. If you do that, everyone in the village will ostracize him. He will be the only person in the village with a place to live. If you want to rebuild one house you need to rebuild the entire village."

I thought I could afford to help one fisherman rebuild his small home, but I wasn't sure I could afford to rebuild the entire village.

"So, what will it cost to rebuild all the destroyed homes?" I ventured.

"About $250,000," the official replied. I was right—I couldn't afford to do that!

So I flew home and got some other people involved: World Vision International, our church, other friends—and we raised the $250,000 needed to rebuild La Carbonera, Mexico.

God calls us to be His instruments to help others. Some people will try to put us down and prevent us from doing what God calls us to do. They (and sometimes we—like me when I first saw the fisherman's picture) will come up with all kinds of excuses and reasons why we are not capable. But our quest is just to keep on listening to the call of God, believing in spite of our imperfections, God is going to use each and every one of us. In spite of our ordinariness, He is going to use us in unexpected and amazing ways.

Keeping an eye on
the journey as a whole
makes the twists and turns
understandable.

Keep Your Eye on the Goal

Though you have not seen him, you love him; and even though you do not see him now, you believe in him and are filled with an inexpressible and glorious joy, for you are receiving the goal of your faith, the salvation of your souls.

—1 Peter 1:8–9

Since his father used a certain learning tool on him when he was a child, John Garmon used it with each of his three children as they came along. It had practical benefits for the task at hand, but John thought it offered even more in terms of life skills—something he desperately wanted each of his children to acquire.

It wasn't rocket science—indeed, it just made common sense. But it was something a child would likely never think to do until taught. And John loved to be the teacher when the time was right with his kids.

The tool involved puzzles. His children were used to the wooden puzzles that come with big, thick pieces which fit into a rectangular frame, the kind where the picture flows out of the puzzle area onto the frame. That overlap helps little ones match up colors and images on the frame with the pieces they're trying to fit together.

But at some point, as the children got a bit older, John would start pulling out puzzles of the jig-saw variety. Indeed, John collected scores of these boxed puzzles over the years, so committed was he to the lessons they provided. That is, they had no frames, no borders, and no guides. He would dump the pieces out on the table and watch his children's reactions. Invariably, until they got *the hang of things, they would be stymied: dozens, scores, or eventually hundreds of small pieces, lying mostly upside down on the table.*

John would help, of course. "Let's start by turning all the pieces right-side up. Then, let's see if we can find groups of colors that go together, or maybe things that might fit together—look, here are two pieces with eyes on them that look like a lion or tiger—and look at those teeth—would this piece go with those eye pieces?"

As every parent knows, this is a great exercise for developing minds. But at some point, John would be ready for the grand "Aha!" Eventually, after letting the children struggle sufficiently, getting perilously close to the giving-up stage as the puzzles got harder, John would produce the top of the puzzle box. It had only happened three times since he and his wife only had three children (and you could only do it once since the kids would thereafter insist on using the puzzle top), but he lived for the moment. The look that came over his children's faces when they caught a glimpse of the big picture was priceless.

The lesson, of course, was obvious: looking at the picture of a completed puzzle makes it far easier to discover where each piece fits.

If the only benefit of the box-top exercise was making the puzzles easier to put together, that would have been enough. But there was more. After several years of learning to use a big picture to put puzzle pieces together it became a metaphor he could use with them in other ways as they got older. If they got a new toy requiring assembly from a bag of parts, they'd use a picture of the completed toy if they got stuck with the instructions. If they were going to plant a small flower garden in the back yard, they'd draw out the colors and schemes before buying seeds and transplants. And if they had to work on a school paper, they'd create a theme and outline before ever starting to write.

John's goal was to teach his children to look at life as a big picture, a theme, a box-top, a landscape. He wanted them to learn that whenever they got stuck with any particular piece of life they would discover where it fit more quickly if they could relate it to the whole. He wanted them to live first at the level of life-as-tapestry, not life-as-knots-and-threads. With the beauty of the finished product to inspire them, they would be far more likely to untie the tangles that would inevitably come.

THEY CALLED HIM THE KID, The Thumper, Teddy Ballgame, and the Splendid Splinter. At least that's what die-hard Boston Red Sox fans called him in the 1940s and '50s. Most of America knew him as Ted Williams, the left fielder who played nineteen years for the BoSox, twice interrupted by military service. Most fans then, and many still today, would argue that Ted Williams was the greatest hitter in the history of baseball.

They could be right. The Thumper led the league in batting six times and won the Triple Crown twice (most home runs, most runs batted in, and highest batting average in a single season). He had a career batting average of .344 with 521 home runs. Even with all those achievements Ted Williams may best be remembered as the last player in Major League Baseball to bat over .400 in a single season: .406 in 1941.

By his own admission, the secret to Ted Williams's success as a hitter was his ability to keep his eye on the ball. In fact, he swore his eyes were so good he could actually see the meeting point of ball and bat—when the ball would go from round to egg-shaped as it made contact with the bat. He had what baseball players refer to as "camera eyes"—the ability to track the ball as it traveled the sixty feet, six inches from the pitcher's mound to home plate. In fact, in a series of stop-action photos of Ted Williams's swing, published in *LIFE* magazine in 1941, the year he hit .406, you can see his eyes focused on the spot where the ball and bat met. Maybe it was true that he had an uncanny ability for keeping his eye on the ball.

Keeping one's eye on the ball in sports is commendable—but it's hardly a matter of life and death. But in naval aviation, it is exactly that. If you're a navy pilot charged with the task of landing a ten-ton jet fighter going 150 miles per hour on an angled 135×20-foot strip of steel on the moving-ahead, heaving deck of an aircraft carrier—in the middle of the night—your ability to keep your eye on the ball takes on a whole new meaning.

When a jet approaches the deck of an aircraft carrier to land, the Landing Signal Officer on the deck will radio the incoming pilot to "call the ball." The "ball" the LSO refers to is a round, orange light reflected through a Fresnel lens on the left side of the deck. The steady, centered position of that ball of light is what will guide the pilot to a safe landing on the deck. When the LSO asks the pilot to "call the ball," the pilot will respond, "I have the ball," meaning he has sighted the ball of light and is using it to home in on the flight deck.

Aircraft carrier decks have minimal amounts of light on them at night. So when a pilot approaches the deck his eyes are fixed on one thing: the ball. Keeping the ball centered and your glide path neither too high nor too low will ensure a three-wire landing—catching the third of the four arresting cables stretched across the deck to catch a jet's tail hook when it lands. At best, carrier landings are risky business—navy pilots call them "controlled crashes." But take your eye off the ball and it could be lights out for good.

My father and I had the opportunity to spend twenty-four hours on the U.S.S. *Ranger* while it was at sea off the coast of California—a U.S. Navy aircraft carrier based in San Diego. And we arrived and departed by air, not by sea. I can only say this: If you got a charge out of the flight-deck scenes in the movie *Top Gun* (which was partially filmed on the U.S.S. *Ranger*), you would have loved actually being there. I was ready to sign on the dotted line and become a Top Gun pilot on the spot!

Not that I would, of course. The men and women who fly the airplanes on and off these flattops have commitment and dedication to spare. The night we spent on the *Ranger* was like every other night on an aircraft carrier—constant takeoffs and landings. The practice never stops. And when I witnessed pilots bringing their screaming warplanes out of a black sky onto a lights-out deck with nothing but faith, skill, and a glowing orange ball to guide them, I got a new appreciation for the difficulty, yet necessity, of keeping one's eye on the ball. It literally is a matter of life and death.

And here's the amazing thing: as soon as a plane hits the deck of the carrier, instead of killing the plane's jet engines the pilot does the opposite—he slams the throttle forward. Why? So in case the plane misses all four of the arresting cables on the deck and continues moving forward its engines will be at full throttle to take it off the carrier and bring it around for another attempt.

There will be times in life when we'll miss a safe landing. But if we are living at full throttle and keeping our eye on the ball, we will land safely in due time.

Calling the Ball

Hoping not to push the metaphor too far, there is a sense in which God is continually saying to us, "Call the ball." We spend our whole life attempting to bring our lives in for a safe landing on what looks like a postage stamp in the middle of the Pacific. God sees us approaching for a landing and radios for us to "call the ball." He's asking us whether we are lined up correctly, whether we're coming in safely, and whether we're going to survive. Or whether we ought to pass and come back around for another approach later.

Think of all the potentially dangerous landings we attempt to make in our lives. We try to choose a life partner. We try to choose a career. We try to decide whether to chuck the assurance of our nine-to-five job and start our own business. We try to help our children make life-determining decisions. We are tempted by gray-area issues and other opportunities we know are just plain wrong. And in all of these major issues, and a thousand other less-critical ones, God is saying, "Call the ball! Make sure you can see your way clear to a safe landing with this choice you are making. If you can't call the ball, don't commit. The results may be catastrophic if you do."

What is "the ball" in our lives? Unfortunately, we don't have a glowing orange ball moving out ahead of us guiding us to a safe landing. But there are other indicators we can use. First, lots of areas can be settled easily by turning to Scripture. There's nothing naïve or simplistic about the old fundamentalist saying, "The Bible says it, I believe it, and that settles it." When the Bible speaks clearly about life overall ("whatever you do, do it all for the glory of God" [1 Cor. 10:31]), or individual issues on which we must make decisions ("You shall not commit adultery" [Ex. 20:14]), it is a pretty reliable ball on which to keep one's eye glued.

In this book, however, we're talking about something bigger and harder to isolate; something the Bible doesn't speak to on an individual basis: finding one's purpose in life. In that case, our ball becomes more like the top of a jigsaw puzzle box—a picture or an idea of how we want our lives to look; a picture with a thousand different pieces, all of which need to fit together to create the life we are trying to live.

In that case, when God says, "Call the ball," and we say, "I have the ball," what we mean is, "I see the picture . . . I know where I'm heading . . . I'm locked into a path that is going to result in a safe landing today and tomorrow until the end of my life."

Unfortunately, the path through life is rarely straight. Like the deck of a tossing aircraft carrier in a storm, it is a moving target on which we have to attempt to stay fixed.

Jigsaw puzzles have become an annual vacation tradition for our family, and one I recommend for a variety of reasons. We've been blessed through the years to have access to a condominium in a lovely beach setting. We block out two weeks every year for our family to get away and unwind.

After arriving and getting settled, it's not long before we pull out one of the many difficult puzzles stored at the condo and dump it on a table—and there it sits, multiplying in size like some multi-cell organism, until the last piece is clicked into place. Sometimes at night the whole family works on it together. Other times, one or two people will stand over the table for a few minutes and make a contribution.

Eventually, when the puzzle is done—whether it takes a day or a week—it goes back in the box and another is dumped out in its place. When we're on vacation there is a never-ending round of puzzles to solve.

Life is like that too—a never-ending supply of puzzles to solve. It's just the way things are. And it's what makes life challenging and exciting. Just as our vacations are made more enjoyable by our host's supply of jigsaw puzzles, so life is as well by the puzzles we're called on to solve.

No Straight Streets

It's been my privilege to lead a dozen or more tours to the Holy Land through the years. And Christians familiar with the story of Saul of Tarsus' conversion are always interested to discover that "the street which is called Straight" (Acts 9:11 KJV) in Damascus really is straight.

The ancient city of Damascus, in Syria, due north of Israel, had a central artery running through it called Straight Street. It was rare for an ancient city to have such a street. Most of the streets, especially in cities like Jerusalem that were razed and rebuilt scores of times throughout history, were narrow and crooked, not unlike the streets in some modern cities. But Damascus' Straight Street ran from one side of the city to another, one hundred feet wide with the equivalent of a modern sidewalk along each side. Calling the ball when approaching Straight Street would have been a piece of cake.

Unfortunately, life is not like Straight Street. Like the proverbial distance from point A to point B, life is not a straight line. Instead, life is more like Lombard Street in San Francisco, reputed to be the "twistiest," most crooked street in America, if not the world. San Francisco is famous for its hilly streets, but Lombard won the prize for being a treacherous drive until it was re-engineered to make it safer. Starting at the top of Lombard, after it crosses Hyde Street, and until it reaches Leavenworth Street, the cross-street at the bottom, Lombard Street is like a downhill roller-coaster ride.

To keep Lombard from being a one-way, death-defying drop toward the San Francisco Bay, the formerly straight street was given a series of hairpin S-curves within the space of one city block. Low, walled gardens were built, projecting from the sides of the street into the center, creating four right-hand and four left-hand S-curves—a total of eight from top to bottom. Maximum speed on the one-way, downhill street is now around five to ten miles per hour. And you spend as much time going sideways as you do going downhill. But at least you arrive at the bottom in one piece.

A road that has Lombard Street beat for curves is called "24-Zig," which stands for the twenty-four zigzag turns the road makes in the space of 2.4 miles—one S-curve every one-tenth of a mile. "24-Zig" was part of the then-famous Burma Road, the 670-mile-long road carved by 200,000 Chinese laborers through the Burmese (now Myanmar) and Chinese mountainous jungles in the late 1930s. The Burma Road was used to transport supplies and armaments from Burma to China to support the Chinese defense against Japanese invaders.

The only remaining historical photograph of the "24-Zig" makes it look like a long piece of spaghetti laid out with twenty-four perfect, near-symmetrical hairpin turns running along the top of the mountain ridges. It appears one might travel ten miles in order to traverse the 2.4 miles of the "24-Zig"—most of it spent going sideways.

If you're like me, you may sometimes feel you are traveling ten miles to go two miles—the old "two steps forward, one step back" routine. That's because life has no straight streets. The road from womb to tomb is full of hairpin turns from start to finish. That's why the overview is the best view.

I'm still looking for straight streets in life. So far, my conclusion is they are few and far between. For instance, I've visited enough people in hospitals and spoken with enough doctors to know that, when it comes to healing from a serious disease or injury, the path is never straight. There is recovery and there are setbacks; there is progress and there is regression. And all of it takes time and patience.

I injured my back over the last Christmas holiday and am still feeling the effects nearly two months later. Yes, it's getting better, but it hasn't been a straight path. It's been two steps forward and one step back, so gradually I'm approaching normal. Sometimes I think God uses these disruptive processes in our physical lives to remind us the spiritual life is similar.

If you're a crow, you can fly from point A to point B in a straight line. But we don't walk as the crow flies. Our path is rarely a straight line.

The Overview Is the Best View

If you want to get a good visual image of what life is like, take an aerial view of Lombard Street in San Francisco. Use Google's "map" function to call up the street and use the "satellite" view, zooming in to the tightest resolution, and you'll see a perfect photo of Lombard Street's twists and turns. To view the historical image of "24-Zig" go to the Web site of CBI Expeditions (http://www.cbiexpeditions.com/html_pages/article2.htm).

It helps to get above life at times and look down from the vantage point of the sky—or the vantage point of heaven, to be more accurate. When looking down on Lombard Street or "24-Zig" you can see point A and point B—the beginning and the end. But what if you were at the midpoint of either of these two roads, going sideways toward the next turn? You'd have no way of knowing that moving laterally was the only way to continue moving forward. Unless you had the overview.

When you and I are going through life we often think we're moving perpendicular to our intended destination. And often we are! But the truth is, from heaven's perspective—from the perspective of the overview—it's the only way to get where we want to go. That's why knowing what the top of the box looks like, the top that has the picture we're trying to put together from the pieces, is imperative. Without that picture or image of who we are and what we're trying to accomplish it's easy to conclude we've gotten off the path.

It would be nice to enter our name in the Google Maps search engine and come up with an overview of our life. In lieu of that nonexistent option, how do we create an overview and keep it before us as a reference? By taking time to create it ourselves. And we do that by reflection, prayer, counseling, evaluating our history, and consulting with those we trust. In essence, by creating the kind of life-map I mentioned in chapter two.

Unfortunately, we rarely take the time to do that kind of planning and reflection. As a result, we are often not sure where we are heading. (More on this below.)

Draw Your Own Map

When it comes to creating our own overview—our own assessment of who we are and where we're going—there are lots of things we can do. From the Bible's point of view, step one is not "Know thyself" as Socrates (and others have) said. Instead, it is to know God. It is only in knowing God that we can know ourselves. He is like a mirror bouncing back a reflection not of who we are but of who we were created to be. In God, and more specifically in Christ Himself, see the image of who we are destined to become.

So that's the first place to begin. But because looking into the face of God is a deep and thoughtful process, we are often tempted to look around and find someone with a life we would like to emulate, even duplicate. We think, *Why not just get on the path they've already carved out? If it worked for them, it will work for me.* Wrong.

In the introduction to this book I mentioned the realization I came to in my own life, which is what prompted the writing of this book. Growing up under the influence of my father, an internationally respected pastor and church leader, I knew I could either take the easy path or the more challenging path. I could either become a mirror image of my father—walk in his shoes—or find shoes of my own. The latter was what I chose because it was the only path with integrity. And the same is true for you. No one in this world has lived the path and purpose God created you to live. You cannot adopt anyone else's life or lifestyle for your own. It is an unsustainable way to live. The only life God has given you the resources to live is your own.

And this isn't always easy. You may recall in the book of Acts how Paul and Barnabas set off on their first missionary journey with Barnabas's cousin, John Mark, as their assistant. Just before they entered what would become the most dangerous leg of the journey John Mark bailed. We don't know why—the Bible said he just left (see Acts 13:13). When Paul and Barnabas got ready for their second journey, Barnabas wanted John Mark to accompany them again, but Paul said, "No way." Some have criticized Paul for being unwilling to give John Mark a second chance. Be that as it may, here's a better lesson: There are few things in life that can be duplicated. Just because John Mark was with them on the first journey didn't mean he needed to be there on the second. So Paul stuck to his guns and chose Silas as his new companion while Barnabas and John Mark went a different direction.

No harm, no foul. Instead of judging what we don't know, let's apply the lesson that just because a particular path in life worked for one person doesn't mean it will work for you. You and I need to create our own path, our own purpose, our own overview, our own direction.

Take Time to View the Forest

Most people in America are familiar with Bill Gates—he's been the world's richest person for more than a decade. Ninety-five percent of the computers in the world run on software sold by the company he cofounded. When he was CEO of Microsoft he had an annual ritual called "Two Weeks in the Woods." He would take a laptop computer, enough food to last, and boxes and boxes of reading material—books, magazines, and research on science, medicine, technology, culture, business—and retreat to a cabin in the woods.

The purpose of these retreats was to refresh himself on the world and his and Microsoft's place in it; to step away from the trees and try to look at the forest as a whole. Only then could he ask and answer the two questions every business—and every individual—ought to ask on a regular basis: 1) What business am I in? 2) How's business? While on his retreat he would type up notes on what he was learning and thinking, and distribute them to his leadership team when he returned. Those notes then became the basis for further discussion on the company and its mission in the coming year.

When is the last time you stepped off the path of your life to assess the direction in which you are headed? Without doing that periodically it's hard to prove to anyone the path we are on is the one we should be on. We need the confirming benefits of reflection, prayer, study, and questioning in order to live a life of confidence.

Times of retreat and reflection are like the work a highway maintenance crew does on an ongoing basis. They find and repair potholes and test and reinforce guardrails to keep travelers safe. When we draw aside and examine our values, beliefs, and practices we're doing the same things. When we go around the S-curves and hairpin turns on life's road, our values, beliefs, and practices keep us from going over the cliff. And if you haven't examined those recently you may need to take time to look at them afresh.

I encourage you to plan time to get away and look at the forest as a whole. Take the top to your puzzle box with you and make sure the pieces of your life are lining up and interlocking where they should.

Work Smart, then Hard

I'm a firm believer in hard work. After all, it's the American way. But there's something wrong with the idea that hard work is the be all and end all of a successful life. If hard work were the only key, every construction worker, factory worker, coal miner, and lumberjack in the world would be millionaires. There's something else that has to accompany hard work—and that something is smart work.

I have a friend who painted houses all his life. He charged twenty dollars an hour for his labor and because he was self-employed he had no benefits. Everything he needed—medical care, vacations, retirement—he had to provide for himself. But he lived in a comfortable home and always put money away for a "rainy day" and retirement. The rainy day and retirement came at the same time, and sooner than he thought, due to a stroke. So he had to stop work and rely on the proceeds from his hard work and smart planning through the years.

Today he has an income property in Texas, a very comfortable home in Southern California, an oceanfront home in the Philippines, and a nice boat to enjoy. He said, "I never dreamed I would have it this good." How did a self-employed house painter who had to pay his own way his entire life end up in such a happy situation when he was forced to retire? He didn't win the lottery. Instead, he worked hard and smart his entire life. For thirty-five years he put away 10 percent of his income into savings. He took advantage of what financial analysts refer to as the "eighth wonder of the world"—the power of compounding interest.

What my friend knew is that it's impossible to outsmart life. If we don't work, save, and plan for the future it will be unreasonable to expect the future to provide for our needs. The book of Proverbs is full of common-sense admonitions to live reasonably. And the same is true with regard to the spiritual side of life: We will not outsmart God. If we try to create and live a life for ourselves outside God's parameters and guidelines, we will not succeed in the long run.

As part of the reflection I encouraged above, ask yourself this question: "Am I attempting to do an end-run around God's best for my life?" If you are, may I encourage you to consider getting on a path He can support and bless? No one—not you and not me—can outsmart God. The beginning of wisdom and knowledge is to fear (honor and respect) Him (see Prov. 1:7).

Think Long Before Short

I'm going to conclude this chapter with a story about how I was reminded to take the long view of life instead of the short. I count it as a watershed moment in my life—a time at which I might have fallen off God's path for my life had it not been for the wisdom of a godly man.

My first marriage ended when my wife of nine years filed for a divorce. I was devastated by her decision, but not just personally. I was pastoring a church I founded and couldn't help but believe this event might signal the end of my ministry. I have written in other books more about the events that ensued, but here I want to recount a discussion I had with my father. He was brokenhearted for me, of course, when I shared the news of my wife's decision. But through his tears he related the following story that saved my life.

A good friend of ours, a pastor in another denomination, found himself divorced after only two years of marriage. My dad reminded me of just how devastated our friend felt when this happened. He thought the same thing I was thinking—his pastoral ministry was probably over. Our friend went to see a bishop in his denomination for counsel and poured out his heart to the older saint. The bishop let our friend finish his story and then told him he had two options: "You can fulfill the ministry and call God has given you, or you can quit and walk away. It's that simple."

When I heard those words it was if God Himself spoke them to me. The bishop who ministered to our friend might as well have been sitting there talking directly to me. All I can tell you is that today, twenty-three years after my father told me that story, I am still in the pastoral ministry. I realized that day, and in the weeks and months following, that I knew the overview of my life. My divorce, though not of my own doing, almost slung me off one of those hairpin turns we go around in life. But when I reconsidered what I believed God called me to do, I had no option but to keep going.

Keep your eye on the ball. Don't look for straight streets and don't fear going sideways when you have to. Develop an overview and create your own personal map. Step back and look at the forest. Work smart as well as hard. And whatever you do, live life like a marathon, not a sprint.

We are immortal beings,
created for eternity.
Therefore, the journey is our
never-ending destination.

The Journey Is the Destination

Your eyes saw my unformed body. All the days ordained for me were
written in your book before one of them came to be.

—Psalm 139:16

Terry Miller and his wife were both self-employed, he a writer and she a graphic designer. Given their ability to live and work any place with broadband Internet connectivity, they decided to pull up roots and move. Having lived in Boston for seven years they decided to turn the tables and move to the West Coast.

Then came a writing proposal from Terry's publisher. Terry was an experienced regional travel writer and photographer, having produced books and articles on New England that were well received. He had a knack for finding and taking the back roads and discovering aspects of an area that seemed on the verge of disappearing—and writing about them in an engaging style. Now his publisher wanted Terry to apply his skills to an expanded target—a book on vanishing aspects of "Americana."

When he and his wife discussed the book proposal, it seemed to dovetail nicely with their desire for a change in scenery in their personal lives. That's when it hit them: Why not drive across America from Boston to San Francisco and do research for the book on the way? They had to get to San Francisco somehow—with some planning and an extended itinerary, they could do two things at once.

Terry's goal was to write a book about the back roads of America. In order to accomplish that goal he would need to drive those back roads. For this project, the journey became the destination. By the time he and Annie arrived in San Francisco, the goal would have been met. Yes, he would still need to write the book—but the majority of the research would have been done.

In due course, they packed up their belongings and had them shipped and stored in San Francisco to await their arrival. They sold one of their cars, keeping their small van, and started plotting their eight-week journey along America's veins and arteries. They would follow the Appalachian Mountains south to North Carolina, dip into Georgia, and head west toward Texas. From there it would be north through the heartland, a left turn in Minnesota until they hit mid-Montana, then south to Arizona and up through central California to the Bay area. That would leave the Northwest area to be explored once they were settled in San Francisco.

In a conversation with his publisher after getting settled in San Francisco, Terry reflected on the "journey as destination" idea:

"Because I'm a travel writer, the idea of a journey being tied so closely with a product is natural for me. But Annie had the same response even though her graphic design work isn't related to travel. She realized, after driving for eight weeks across America, that she was a different artist than the one who left Boston. She saw things differently. Colors, shapes, textures, people—they're different wherever you go. By living in one region of the country for so long we had allowed our 'journey' to set the limits for our imagination, and thus our products. I know I will be a different writer, and Annie a different artist, because of our journey. But I believe we will also be better. How could we not be?"

"I think you should explore that idea when you begin to write," Terry's publisher responded. "Think of America as a person who has been, at least since 1776, on a 230-year journey. What are we except the sum total of two-plus centuries of experiences? It's not like our country, or any country, has a destination to which we're headed. Barring calamities, America's future, like every nation's, is open-ended. That alone suggests the journey itself is the destination."

"Not to get too metaphysical here," Terry replied, "but I guess that could also be said of individuals. We tend to think of our lives ending when we die, and therefore think of something we do in our productive adult years as the 'goal' of our lives. But what if, as most religions teach, life goes on after death. That means we're immortal, or eternal, and that our personal journey becomes our destination as well—one that goes on forever."

N 1967, A SEVENTEEN-YEAR-OLD high school graduate went for a swim in the Chesapeake Bay with her sister. It was a routine summer outing, something to enjoy before heading to college in September. Swimming out to a raft just offshore, Joni Eareckson pulled herself onto it and then dove off into what she thought was deep water. But her head hit the bottom and her neck snapped back, crushing her fourth cervical vertebra and immediately paralyzing her. Conscious, but floating face-down in the water and unable to move, she could only hope her sister would see her.

Kathy Eareckson was walking in the shallow water, heading for shore with her back to the raft, when a crab bit her on the toe. She turned to call out to Joni to warn her about the crabs and saw Joni's blond hair floating just beneath the surface of the water. She rushed to her sister's aid and pulled her face out of the water so she could breathe and then pulled Joni to shore.

Thus began one of the most amazing journey-as-destination stories in modern times. Joni Eareckson's (now Joni Eareckson Tada) story is so well known to people of my generation, that I'm hesitant to repeat it. Indeed, she appeared on our own internationally broadcast television program, *The Hour of Power*, several times in the years following her injury. But Joni is now in her mid-fifties, and many younger people are not as familiar with her story. And it is a story everyone should know. Joni's thirty-five books, her ministry's Web site (joniandfriends.org), and a 1980 motion picture of her life story make the details of her injury and rehabilitation accessible to all.

But this part of Joni's life story is always worth retelling: It has been her journey as a quadriplegic that has given birth to a life message which has touched the lives of millions of people around the world. Very few people have traveled a more fruitful journey—even those not confined to a wheelchair without use of their hands or arms—than Joni. Her many titles include author, singer-songwriter, artist (painting by holding the paintbrush in her teeth), actor, public speaker, radio broadcaster, and advocate for the disabled around the world. Joni has received five honorary academic degrees and received numerous awards from Christian and non-Christian organizations for her public service on behalf of the disabled.

While her energies on behalf of the disabled are without respect to culture or creed, underlying everything she does is a life-message that Jesus Christ, as Lord of creation and Lord of her life, knows what's best.

The same question we have about the way our lives have developed is easy to ask about Joni: would she have accomplished all the same things had she not become a quadriplegic? And the answer, of course, is unknowable. We only know in life what has happened, not what might have happened. And what we do know about Joni's journey is that it has become her destination. She has become a spokeswoman for the grace and power of God—and that is something she wasn't before her accident.

In a 2004 interview with television host Larry King, Joni told how it takes six to eight months, even as much as a year, to finish a single painting because of the tedium of painting "by mouth" instead of with her hands. When King asked whether or not that required a lot of patience, Joni responded, "Well, that's the bruising of a blessing of this disability, Larry. I just don't think I would be as persevering, I don't think I would be as patient. I don't think I would care about other peoples' needs. But this wheelchair, I think, has been God's way of turning my life inside out, and jerking my priorities and values right side up."

She also told King about what she anticipates saying to Jesus Christ one day in heaven: "You were right, when you said [that] in this world we would have trouble. And there's a lot of trouble being a quadriplegic, but you know what, the weaker I was in that thing, the harder I leaned on you and the harder I leaned on you, the stronger I discovered you to be. Thank you for the bruising of a blessing it was, this severe mercy. Thank you." (Reference if needed: http://transcripts.cnn.com/TRANSCRIPTS/0408/03/lkl.00.html.)

Values . . . priorities . . . caring about other peoples' lives . . . depending on God. Those could easily be "destinations" all of us aspire to attain. But for Joni, it was the journey that created the destination. Yes, she might have reached those goals another way. But the point is, she agreed to develop them the way God gave her—on the journey God set before her launching when she was seventeen years old and has continued to this day as a quadriplegic in a wheelchair.

Joni's journey is obviously different from most peoples'. I have made reference to hers because it's a dramatic example of how something that happens one day in our life can be the first step in a journey lasting a lifetime; and how that journey can become a destination that continues to unfold like the petals on a flower. The farther we travel on the journey, the more dimensions the destination takes on.

We often use the phrase "When I . . ." Young people say, "When I grow up I'm going to . . ." Young adults say, "When I finish school I'm going to . . ." And adults say, "When I get promoted I'm going to . . ." There's nothing wrong with that kind of thinking, of course. But it does reflect our preoccupation with the future as a destination or place of accomplishment. In truth, the future will be no different from today. Unless we learn to live in the present moment of the journey God has planned for our lives, we will always live with the grass-is-greener mentality.

I have already said in a previous chapter the Christian's destination, or ultimate purpose in life, is Christlikeness (see Romans 8:29). And it's easy to think death is the destination that transforms us into Christ's image when we finally go to heaven. But God is using the journey as the destination. He is transforming us every step of the way, conforming us to Christ's likeness day-by-day. Yes, our transition to heaven completes the process. But you and I need to embrace the place in our journey where we are right now. Because the journey is the destination.

Do You Believe in Miracles?

In 1980, young sportscaster Al Michaels shouted those words to the television audience who just witnessed a college-aged United States hockey team defeat a veteran Soviet hockey team—the best in the world—at the Winter Olympic Games in Lake Placid, New York. He not only asked the question—"Do you believe in miracles?"—he answered it by shouting, "Yes!"

The seven months leading up to, and including, that unpredictable victory were chronicled in the wonderful 2004 motion picture *Miracle*. It was the story of how the American coach, Herb Brooks, cobbled together an Olympic hockey team from America's best college players and taught them a new style of hockey, a style that would match and defeat the Soviets. The last time the United States had beaten the Soviets in hockey was 1960. The Soviets won every Olympic gold medal thereafter: '64, '68, '72, and '76 until 1980.

In that incredible story of victory in 1980 are all the elements that illustrate how the journey is the destination. Yes, defeating the Soviet team in the Olympic semifinal game in February 1980 and then going on to defeat Finland and win gold in the finals, was the destination Herb Brooks had in mind. But the journey leading up to that point—at least as portrayed in *Miracle*—contained enough climactic elements to make the journey worthwhile regardless the final outcome.

As I highlight a number of instances from the movie about the "miracle team," don't overanalyze my comparisons. This isn't a spiritual movie, and I'm not using Coach Brooks to represent God nor the players to represent Christians. This isn't a divine parable. But just as Jesus often used images and situations from life to make spiritual points, we can do the same with this story.

The Right, Not the Best

A couple hundred young hockey players gathered for the Olympic team tryouts, and on the first day Herb Brooks, the coach, handed a list to his assistant, Craig Patrick, with twenty-six names on it, from which a team of twenty would be chosen. Craig looked at the list, astonished that Herb had already chosen his players.

CRAIG: You're missing some of the best players.

HERB: I'm not looking for the best players, Craig. I'm looking for the right ones.

Years ago I saw a hilarious piece that someone wrote, posing as a management consultant, providing feedback to Jesus on the "leadership team" (the twelve disciples) He assembled for His new venture. The twelve disciples—fishermen, "sons of thunder," a thief, a tax collector, and other rag-tags from the backwaters of Galilee—were hardly what one would call "the best." But they were the right ones.

If you have begun a journey following Jesus of Nazareth, it's because you were chosen (see 1 Thess. 1:4). And you were chosen according to God's own purposes and plan. Don't try to figure it out. Just rest in the knowledge that your journey with Jesus is your destiny.

No Getting Off Easy

At the end of the week's tryout session, Craig Patrick gathered the entire group together and read off the names of the twenty-six who had made the cut. As the disappointed ones left the scene, Coach Brooks spoke to those who remained.

HERB: Take a good look, gentlemen, because they're the ones getting off easy.

Sometimes I wonder if the twelve disciples of Jesus would have stayed around in the early days had they known what was coming. They had visions of a glorious kingdom to be set up with Jesus as the Messiah and them sitting on His right and left hand in places of authority and importance (see Matt. 20:21). "All in good time; all in good time," Jesus might have replied, truthfully (see Matt. 19:28).

And when a number of His followers decided to turn away from following Him (see John 6:66), I wonder if He would have said something to the Twelve similar to what Coach Brooks told his starry-eyed recruits: "They're the ones getting off easy."

The apostle Paul was up-front with a number of new converts in Asia Minor when he told them, "We must go through many hardships to enter the kingdom of God" (Acts 14:22). The hardships are part of the journey. There is no destination without them.

Chosen for a Reason

When one of the sponsoring officials of the USA Olympic hockey team chastised Herb Brooks for choosing the team members alone, without input from others, he responded firmly.

> HERB: I already know my team. . . . Every one of these boys was chosen for a specific reason. I've studied film on each and every one of these boys. I've watched them. And I've coached a lot of them. And the ones I haven't, I've spoken with their coaches and scouts in the area. Now I know best what I need to compete. And the team I've chosen is it.

If you want to see how well God knows you, read Psalm 139:14–16. And if you want to see with what care God chose you "for a reason," read Paul's description of how spiritual gifts were given to individual believers: "All these [spiritual gifts] are the work of one and the same Spirit, and he gives them to each one, just as he determines. . . . But in fact God has arranged the parts in the body, every one of them, just as he wanted them to be" (1 Cor. 12:11, 18).

You have had a part to play on God's "team" since the day you were chosen by Him; since the day you became a Christian. That means the future is now—the journey is the destination.

Methods in the Madness

After working with the players, getting them in shape for the Olympics, assistant coach Craig Patrick became concerned about how hard Herb Brooks was pushing the players. He went to "Doc," the team doctor and trainer who had worked with Herb for years.

> CRAIG: Hey, Doc, let me ask you a question, all right? You've worked with Herb for a long time, right?

> DOC: Oh, I've known Herb for quite some time.

CRAIG: So tell me something. Does he always treat his players like this?

DOC: No. No, no. This I have never seen. But Craig, believe me. Herb has a reason for everything he does.

Do you ever wonder why God does what He does? I certainly have in my relationship with Him—especially when in pain of various sorts. It is in those times—those stages of my journey—I rely on verses like Ephesians 1:11: "In him we were also chosen, having been predestined according to the plan of him *who works out everything in conformity with the purpose of his will.*"

The apostle Peter once uttered these words: "Surely not, Lord!" (Acts 10:14). Do you see anything contradictory there? How about saying no to someone you consider to be Lord? Part of the purpose of the journey is for us to learn that God has a reason for everything He does.

Lessons in Humility

Herb's obsession with building the Olympic hockey team began to create tension in his marriage. His wife, Patty, began to resent the lack of time he spent with the family. When her resentment finally spilled over one night, Herb realized he had charged into his mission without ever talking over with Patty what would be required. He never asked her if she was willing to travel down a difficult road with him. He went to her to apologize.

HERB: I'm sorry we didn't talk. And I was wrong not to ask. So I'm asking now if you—you know, if you can be with me on this, because it won't mean anything if you're not.

We're on this journey of redemption as Christians because we need to be redeemed from our selfish and sinful ways. And we can fully expect to have to eat a measured amount of humble pie along the way. Apologies, confessions, requests to be forgiven—from others as well as God—are part of the journey. They are our daily reminders of how great is the grace that saves and forgives us. And how much we need it. And we find that God does, indeed, honor those willing to humble themselves (see James 4:6).

Trained for Triumph

When Herb introduced his team to the kinds of conditioning sprints they'd be doing on the ice, he held nothing back.

> HERB: Get used to this drill. We'll be doing it a lot. Why? Because the legs feed the wolf, gentlemen. I can't promise you will be the best team at Lake Placid next February. But we will be the best conditioned. That I can promise you. . . . Be prepared to grow through pain, gentlemen. You're going to skate harder than you've ever skated in your lives every minute of every day you're on the ice with me.

Ouch! Herb Brooks was nothing if not honest. He knew that until the basic conditioning exercises were embraced as a necessary part of their seven-month journey, victory wasn't even a destination to be considered. If you could have asked his players the day they won gold at Lake Placid whether the training regimens were worth it, what do you think they would have said?

There's a reason the basics of the Christian life—prayer, Bible study, service, worship, scripture memory and meditation, and others—are called spiritual disciplines. They are the daily steps on the journey that make the destination possible. It's why Paul once wrote to Timothy to "train yourself to be godly" (1 Tim. 4:7).

Failure by Intimidation

At a film session, Herb showed the Soviet team in action, while his young players sat in silent awe of what they were seeing.

> HERB: Their main weapon is intimidation. They know they're going to win. And so do their opponents. . . . Everybody in this room knows what people are saying about our chances. I know it. You know it. But I also know there is a way to stay with this [Soviet] team. . . . The rest of the world is afraid of them. Boys, we won't be. No one has ever worked hard enough to skate with the Soviet team for an entire game. Gentlemen, we are going to work hard enough.

How many times do you and I forfeit a victory on the basis of intimidation alone? We defeat ourselves mentally before ever walking out the door. "You're not good enough. You're not smart enough. You're not attractive enough. You're not educated enough. You're not strong enough." And on and on, one lie after another we choose to believe. Straight from the mouth of the "father of lies" (John 8:44) comes intimidation designed to convince us we will never be first.

The journey is designed to teach us the difference between intimidation and truth. To learn that difference is to snatch victory from the jaws of defeat before the game even begins.

Permanent Identity

Herb cut the twenty-six-man roster down to twenty-one. He agonized over making the final cut to get the team to twenty. When he decided to cut a player named Ralph, he called him in to his office.

HERB: You're a [heck] of a hockey player. This doesn't change that.

Ralph wouldn't have made it to the list of twenty-one if he hadn't been an excellent hockey player. So his skills weren't the issue. What was at issue was how he might respond to being cut. And Herb reminded him that his being cut did not change the fact he was a great player.

I'm bothered when I hear Christians say, "I'm just a sinner saved by grace." No, according to more than forty verses in the New Testament you are a saint who sometimes still sins. Your identity changed completely when you became a follower of Jesus Christ: from sinner to saint. And the fact you may stumble on your journey doesn't change that fact. God looks at you now the same way He will look at you in heaven: in Christ. And nothing you do, or fail to do, can alter your appearance in His sight. But it takes falling down on the journey a few times to realize it.

Not Shooting the Wounded

A few days before the thirteenth Winter Olympics were to begin, Jack, one of Herb's best players, injured his knee. Herb agonized over whether to keep him on the team in hopes he would recover, or replace him with a previously cut, but healthy, player.

HERB: Jack, I've got twenty guys to think about here, and they're all looking at me to do what's best for this team.

JACK: I understand, Coach.

HERB: Which is why I'm hanging on to you.

All too often we are ready to shoot our wounded—even figuratively shoot ourselves when we fail. In a world where people are treated like commodities or widgets we're used to calling for a replacement whenever someone fails or is "injured" in the line of Christian duty.

But God doesn't. He keeps us on the team. Why? Because the journey is the destination. God would no more kick us off His team now than He would throw us out of heaven once we arrive. Everything God has done in our past is designed to cause us to arrive in a blazing state of glory (see Rom. 8:28–30).

Life Is Your Moment

I want to close this chapter with the words Herb spoke to his players before they went out to face the Soviet team in the semifinal round. And I want to encourage you to read them as if God is speaking them to you—not about a game of hockey but about your very own life. Now is the time for you to embrace the journey to which God has called you. To be excited about heaven and not be excited about every day between now and then is to miss the truth that the journey is the destination.

HERB: Great moments are born of great opportunity. And that's what you have here tonight, boys. That's what you've earned here tonight. One game. If we played [the Soviets] ten times they might win nine. But not this game. Not tonight. Tonight we skate with them. Tonight we stay with them. And we shut them down because we can! Tonight we are the greatest hockey team in the world. You were born to be hockey players. Every one of you. And you were meant to be here tonight. This is your time. Their time is done. It's over. . . . Now go out there and take it!

We see things after making
wrong turns we never
would have seen otherwise.
God uses all of life's events
to shape our identities.

When the Wrong Way Is the Right Way

He gives strength to the weary and increases the power of the weak. Even youths grow tired and weary, and young men stumble and fall; but those who hope in the LORD will renew their strength. They will soar on wings like eagles; they will run and not grow weary, they will walk and not be faint.

—Isaiah 40:29–31

When Rick Busby dropped out of college in the middle of his sophomore year, he did it knowing full well how displeased his parents were. In fact, they told him nicely, but firmly, that if he left college now against their wishes he would have to pay for it himself if he ever decided to re-enroll. But rebellion was in the air and Rick had made up his mind. Good decision or bad, he had to experience the counterculture for himself.

It was 1967 and the "summer of love" was on the horizon. Rick and four friends, two guys and two girls, pooled their meager funds and bought a sort-of-running Volkswagen bus, the quintessential ride of the era. Their destination was not just the city of San Francisco, but the corner of Haight and Ashbury. With their guitars, tie-dyed shirts, army fatigue jackets, bell-bottomed jeans, beads, long hair, and sandals, they headed for hippie heaven. Eventually, over 100,000 young people like themselves would invade the Haight-Ashbury district of San Francisco to "turn on, tune in, and drop out," in the words of guru Timothy Leary.

By the time John Philips of the Mamas and Papas wrote "San Francisco" ("If you're going to San Francisco, be sure to wear some flowers in your hair . . . If you're going to San Francisco, summertime will be a love-in there") the love-in was in full swing. The world's first rock festival, the Monterey Pop Festival, was staged south of San Francisco in June, and Rick and his buddies were there, as stoned as most of the crowd.

At the time, it didn't seem significant, but when the Beatles' album Sgt. Pepper's Lonely Hearts Club Band was released two weeks before the Monterey festival, the title track could have been a requiem for the times. What began as a love-in gradually deteriorated into a quest for meaning and survival. The little money Rick had soon ran out and a couple of his friends gave up and went home in search of good food, a hot shower, and a clean bed. Basically homeless, Rick shuffled from one "pad" to another, looking for anywhere to crash for the night. He scrounged for money and food, trying at least to keep the growls of his empty stomach from drowning out the wails of his lonely heart.

One day word spread through Haight-Ashbury that a concert was going to be sponsored by a movement called the Jesus People. And there would be food. Rick went to feed his body, but unintentionally found something for his soul as well. Instead of talking about getting high on drugs, the speakers and musicians talked about getting high on Jesus. Instead of talking about free sexual love, they talked about the free love of God in Christ. And instead of talking about "no way" when it came to American culture, they talked about "one way" to God through Jesus.

Instead of just eating the free food and then leaving, Rick found himself hanging on the words he was hearing. The peace and contentment on the speakers' faces, and the love in their voices, was something he hadn't seen or heard in months. It stood out in stark contrast to what he concluded was the superficiality of the summer of love. For the first time since arriving in San Francisco, he began to wonder if he'd made a big mistake.

Six months later it was Christmas, and Rick Busby was a different person. He had met Jesus—the Jesus he learned about in years of church but never knew personally. He left San Francisco and moved down to Los Angeles where he got involved in one of many churches reaching out to disillusioned young people. He was baptized in the Pacific Ocean, got a job in *a restaurant and a room in a house with other Christian guys, and began to grow in his walk with Christ.*

A week before Christmas, he did something he hadn't done for almost a year. He called his parents and asked if he could come home.

"I think I made a big mistake," he told them, "dropping out of school against your wishes. That was a rebellious act, and I want you to know I'm sorry. But I also want you to know that something really good has come from it I'd like to tell you about if you'll let me. I've learned some hard lessons, for which I'm thankful. I've got money for bus fare and can be there by the twenty-fourth. Is it okay if I come?"

G OD MADE ME THE MESSENGER of the new heaven and the new earth of which he spoke in the Apocalypse by St. John, after having spoken of it by the mouth of Isaiah; and he showed me the spot where to find it."

Those confident words of Christopher Columbus were written after his third voyage westward from Spain in 1498. He was speaking of what we now call the country of Venezuela, his vantage point being at the mouth of the massive Orinoco River pouring fresh water into the ocean so that it made a "freshwater sea of forty-eight leagues." This long-hypothesized Terrestrial Paradise was the result of the geo-theological theories of the day—that all the inhabited regions of earth were on a single land mass which included Europe, Asia, and Africa.

A little background:

Every schoolchild learns that, "In 1492, Columbus sailed the blue." What they don't learn is that the first-known globe of the world was fashioned that same year. That globe was indeed round—but to see a picture of it reveals a startling omission: the continents of North and South America. From the western coast of Europe to the eastern coast of Asia is nothing but empty ocean.

The Jewish prophetic book 2 Esdras declared that, "On the third day thou didst command the waters to be gathered together in the seventh part of the earth; six parts thou didst dry up and keep so that some of them might be planted and cultivated and be of service before thee" (6:42). This numerical opinion, while not found in the Genesis creation accounts, nonetheless provided Christian cartographers with a foundation for declaring that six-sevenths of the earth's surface was land and one-seventh water. Seven being a divine number, it only made sense that mankind, the pinnacle of God's creation, would be given the preponderance of the earth's surface to live on, cultivate, and domesticate.

In summary, here's what they believed:

- The earth was a sphere.

- Six-sevenths was land and one-seventh was water.

- All the land consisted of Europe, Asia, and Africa.

- Therefore, the one-seventh of water surrounding the six-sevenths of land must allow for a very short distance from the western coast of Europe to the eastern coast of Asia.

Since Columbus, a European, agreed with this geographical perspective, he figured to reach Asia all that was necessary was to sail west across the open water. It was the riches of Asia Europe wanted. Trading by land had been successful ever since the days of Marco Polo who established trade routes from Europe to Asia in the thirteenth century. But when Constantinople, the gateway from Christian Europe to Asia, fell to the Muslims in 1453, trade by land became perilous. Portuguese sailors, led by Vasco de Gama in 1497, learned to sail down the west coast of Africa to reach the Indian Ocean and Asia, but Columbus had a better idea: sail due west from Europe and, voilà!—next stop, Asia!

We know, of course, it never happened. Columbus did find land by sailing west, but it wasn't Asia—it was the islands of today's Caribbean region. On his third voyage (1498), when Columbus bumped into a huge land mass (South America) south of Cuba (which he believed was part of China), the only way to explain its existence, and the bountiful fresh water flowing from it, was to call it Paradise and declare himself the discoverer of it. (What would he have thought had he ventured further south along the coast of South America and encountered the mouth of the mighty Amazon?)

Columbus tried a fourth and final time in 1502 to find what he was looking for. He believed somewhere between Cuba and the Terrestrial Paradise he would find an opening leading into the Indian Ocean. He died in the belief he found the coast of Asia but not the passageway through to the riches of the Indian Ocean region.

People living at the time could only conclude, based on his intentions, Columbus was a failure. What he thought was a good idea turned out not to be. He didn't lack purpose, morals, perseverance, or courage. What he lacked was knowledge and information. He did the best he could—but he failed.

But now, from our vantage point in history, who would dare say Columbus's efforts were a failure? Without his four voyages and the resulting maps and charts he contributed to the science of navigation, would Ferdinand Magellan have succeeded? Another Portuguese explorer, he sailed westward from Spain thirteen years after Columbus's death, continued along the east coast of South America until he rounded the southern tip of that continent, and from there made it across the Pacific Ocean to the Philippine Islands in 1521. Though he was killed there in a battle his crew continued westward until they hit Africa, sailed around the Cape of Good Hope and north to Spain and home in 1522.

Ferdinand Magellan accomplished what Christopher Columbus wanted to. And without Columbus's shoulders to stand on, who's to say he would ever have made it?

Hindsight Is Clear Sight

That history lesson is to communicate the big idea of this chapter: Many wrong turns in life, in retrospect, turn out to be right turns. The problem is not being able to see them that way when they happen. Columbus probably died considering himself a failure to some degree or another. But anyone whose name is used as a marker by historians (for example, "pre-Columbian pottery") can't be considered a failure. It just took longer than his lifetime for Columbus's contribution to be realized.

In chapter two I cited a scripture passage which is another good example of this principle: Exodus 13:17–18. That's the record of how God led the Hebrew slaves out of Egypt to the Promised Land. The Hebrews were given the part of Egypt called Goshen to live in when they first came to Egypt to escape the famine in Canaan—all seventy-odd of them. Goshen was on the eastern edge of Egypt, not far from the curve of the Mediterranean coast as it turns north and becomes the coast of Canaan. If one lived in Goshen and wanted to get to Canaan, a matter of a few days' walk around the coastal trade route would have accomplished the task.

But Moses didn't take the easy route. Instead, from Goshen, after crossing the Red Sea, he turned due south into the desert of Sinai—completely opposite the direction they should have been going to get to Canaan. Did God tell Moses to go this way, or was this Moses' decision? The Bible doesn't say. But what it does say is that the Hebrew slaves ultimately became very unhappy campers with Moses' leadership: Scorching sun, snakes, sand—"What's up with this, Moses?"

But history and hindsight revealed the wisdom of Moses' direction—but not for hundreds of years. The street-fighting Philistines—some of the baddest boys in Canaan (remember Goliath?)—would become a thorn in Israel's side during her early years in the Promised Land. They inhabited the lower coastal region of Canaan—exactly where the Hebrew slaves would have traveled had they taken the coastal route of Goshen.

But thanks to Moses, the Hebrew slaves avoided getting decimated by the Philistines. As bad a decision as it seemed, Moses took them into the desert where they had time to get themselves together as a nation: meet their God, receive their "Constitution" (the Ten Commandments), build their first "church" (the Tabernacle), and exchange their slave mentality for that of God's chosen people. None of that would have happened had they taken the fast-track from Goshen to Canaan.

Moses' choice is another example of a bad decision—a seeming failure in logistics—being the smartest thing they could have done. Whether Moses' decision was intentional or not, we don't know. From a human perspective, it seemed like a bonehead move. But from the perspective of divine wisdom, it couldn't have been more appropriate. It was a nation-saving decision.

Columbus did a good thing that seemed to be a failure but, in hindsight, turned out to pave the way for merchants and explorers who followed him. Moses did a seemingly dumb thing that turned out, in hindsight, to have saved a nation from extinction. And history is filled with other examples of people and incidents like them. But what about times when we want to do something but are prevented, and that turns out to be a good thing? That falls into the "hindsight is clear sight" category as well.

On December 21, 1988, the Motown recording group The Four Tops finished a recording session in London later than they planned. Another English rocker, John Lydon, and his wife Nora missed the same flight because Nora hadn't finished packing in time. A man named Jaswant Basuta had become intoxicated in an airport lounge while waiting for the same flight. When he rushed to the terminal gate the doors had already closed and airline officials refused to delay the plane to let him board. Others had been booked on the flight but supposedly changed their plans at the last minute: a South African foreign minister destined for a U.N. ceremony in New York; the U.S. ambassador to Lebanon; the son of the assistant director of the FBI; a U.S. Drug Enforcement Administration official.

Before Pan American flight 103 took off, each of those individuals had tied their lives and futures to the idea of making that flight. Two hours later, when Pan Am 103 exploded over Lockerbie, Scotland, they realized just the opposite: their lives and futures were theirs because they missed the flight. "The minute we realized what happened, we just looked at each other and almost collapsed," Lydon said later.

I imagine similar stories could be told about every airplane that has ever crashed—people whose lives were saved because they missed the flight. Anger and tears of frustration at missing an airplane flight became tears of joy and inexplicable relief within a matter of hours. Events, whether of our own doing or not, can turn out to be blessings once the passage of time has done its work and revealed its connections. All it takes is a bit of hindsight to recognize that God's plan is bigger than ours; what looks dumb or disastrous or debilitating to us can have an entirely different outcome.

If you want a fabulous look at how connections in life often show up in totally unexpected ways, I commend to you the ten-part documentary television series *Connections* (now available on DVD), authored and hosted by British science historian James Burke, as well as his books. These documentaries have been shown in more than fifty countries and been used in the curricula of hundreds of colleges and universities. Besides all they teach on the history of science and invention, for our purposes they teach this: Don't be too hasty to draw conclusions. You never know where your journey will end, especially when you think you have made a wrong turn in life.

Wrong Turns That Are Our Fault

Let's be honest—we mess up a lot. Much of the time when the journey we call life gets derailed, it's our fault. Perhaps we're undisciplined, lazy, angry, greedy, arrogant, selfish, or self-indulgent, and our dreams fly out the window. It happens to all of us. Often our response is not a response at all—it's a reaction. While the dictionary doesn't make as large a difference between the two words, we have come to understand the difference. A response is thoughtful and measured, while a reaction is impulsive and knee-jerk. It's reacting that I think the apostle James was warning against in James 1:19: "My dear brothers, take note of this: Everyone should be quick to listen, slow to speak and slow to become angry."

I think we tend to react strongly when wrong turns are our fault because we are ashamed and feel guilty. And rightfully so. As the humorist Garrison Keillor once said, "Guilt is the gift that keeps on giving." Pangs of guilt are supposed to move us to consider our ways and repent, not instigate an unhealthy reaction leading only to further wrong turns.

Think about David, the king of Israel. He committed adultery when he should have been out leading his army into battle. He knew what he did was wrong, but instead of responding he reacted—and conspired to have the woman's husband put to death. Now he was guilty of murder as well as adultery (see 2 Sam. 11–12). But, in time, David was restored in his life and went on to be Israel's greatest king—and learned some things along the way (see Ps. 51).

When he was forty years old and a member of the Egyptian royal household, Moses killed an Egyptian in a moment of anger (see Ex. 2). Understandably, he reacted and fled for his life into the desert where he worked as a shepherd for forty years. Then he met God and was invited to be the deliverer of the Hebrew slaves in Egypt. It took forty years, but Moses' wrong turn wasn't permanent. He got back on track in his life and with his God.

A young man named John Mark quit in the middle of accompanying the apostle Paul and his uncle Barnabas on their first missionary journey (see Acts 13). We don't know why, but the tension it caused between Paul and Barnabas, as well as the language in the Greek text of Acts, suggested this was a defection, not a planned departure. Yet, who would have thought? John Mark, years later, was found to be one of Paul's most trusted companions (see 2 Tim. 4:11).

Sometimes wrong turns end badly, as in Judas's case. I think Judas could have been restored had he not been so wracked with guilt that he hanged himself (see Matt. 27:5).

If the Bible says anything, it says our wrong turns are not ours to figure out alone. God sees every one of them and is willing to work with us to get us back on track. I couldn't begin to count the stories I've heard through the years of people whose wrong turns were their fault, but who ended up in a good, or often better, place in spite of themselves. And when that happens, they always know God better than they did before.

Wrong Turns That Are Not Our Fault

If we react badly when wrong turns are our fault out of guilt and shame, we react badly when they're not our fault out of anger: "How could he have done that to me?" "I've served this company faithfully for twenty years. I think I deserve better." "I have loved her faithfully and this is what I get in return?"

Granted, there are no "innocent parties" in life. No one has contributed perfectly to a relationship or an employer or a marriage. But given that understanding, there are times when our journey is thrown into the ditch;

there are times when we are forced to take a wrong turn when it's not our fault. And our natural tendency is to react—and often react badly.

While we'll never be able to say with 100 percent honesty, "It wasn't my fault," there is One who could. And from Him we can learn a few things about how God resurrects wrong turns. Jesus' journey was one of kingship of His people. As the Son of David, He was to inherit the throne of His ancestor and rule over God's people. But through no fault of His own, His journey seemed to take a wrong turn. He was killed for no good reason, executed as a common criminal on a cruel cross.

His disciples certainly thought it was a wrong turn. They mourned His death. One of them said, "We had hoped that he was the one who was going to redeem Israel" (Luke 24:21). But from God's perspective, was Jesus' death a wrong turn? Only if you consider becoming the Lamb of God who takes away the sin of the world a mistake (see John 1:29).

Before you say, "Yes, but that was Jesus," think of what I have said already in this book. God's purpose for your life is to make you Jesus' brother or sister for eternity (see Rom. 8:29). God may not raise you from the dead like He did Jesus, but He will do whatever it takes to keep you on the path leading you to your ultimate destination in life. From Jesus you can learn to respond like He did: "When they hurled their insults at him, he did not retaliate; when he suffered, he made no threats. Instead, he entrusted himself to him who judges justly" (1 Pet. 2:23).

You will take some wrong turns in life that aren't your fault. But if you will entrust yourself to God you will find yourself in a deeper and wiser place than you could have anticipated.

Wrong Turns That Are Nobody's Fault

Sometimes we take wrong turns—turns that interrupt our journey—when they are nobody's fault. Insurance companies call them "acts of God," finding it easier to blame Him when there is no one else to whom responsibility can be assigned. Floods, hurricanes, tornados, fires, natural disasters, some diseases, birth defects, mental impairments—these are things that happen in life no one can explain.

The apostle Paul suffered from such an "act of God"—an undefined "thorn in his flesh" (see 2 Cor. 12). Yes, the Bible says it was a "messenger of Satan"—but we don't know what that means. Whatever the thorn was, Paul apparently saw it as a significant hindrance to his ministry and he asked God three times to remove it. And God said no. But instead of taking something away from Paul, God gave him something to compensate. And God will give you and me the same thing when we take a wrong turn we never saw coming: grace in abundance.

What God said to Paul He says to us: "My grace is sufficient for you, for my power is made perfect in weakness" (v. 9). It is that power we need when we take wrong turns in life—power to get back on our journey. And it is the experience of God's power that makes us learn not to fear wrong turns in life, especially those that are inexplicable.

The next time you find yourself off the road—regardless of who is at fault—listen for words like these coming from your own mouth:

"Why did . . .?"

"Why didn't . . .?"

"Why couldn't . . .?"

"Why can't . . .?"

"If only I . . ."

"If only he/she/they . . ."

"If only God . . ."

Those words are normal and understandable at the outset, but hopefully not ongoing. If you will open your eyes and your heart, I believe you will see things after making a wrong turn you hadn't seen before, including a fresh and different view of God. It is the reality that we can never exhaust the love, mercy, and grace of God which ultimately gives us hope when we are in a hard place. And gives us the desire, regardless the difficulty or time involved, to resume our journey.

Respond instead of reacting. Give things time. Give *God* time. What you see as a failure, an injustice, or a disaster may end up being a right turn in the long term.

We do not walk on this journey alone. God walks and works with us to keep us on course and provide everything we need.

A Divine GPS

For in him we live and move and have our being.

—Acts 17:28

Melanie just turned sixteen a month ago, got her driver's license, and was being allowed to use one of the family cars for limited social excursions. Only one other friend in the car, no talking on the cell phone while driving, no side trips not previously agreed upon, and home by 11:00 p.m.—those were the rules she and her parents established as a means of helping her stay safe until she grew more confident behind the wheel. And so far, she had kept them faithfully. So far.

When she arrived home that night—she had driven to a friend's house to hang out with a few girlfriends—her father was still up. And he didn't look particularly happy.

"How'd it go, sweetie?" her dad said, lowering the TV sound with the remote. "Everything go okay with the car?"

"Yep, everything went fine. I'm getting better all the time at my driving. I even parked by the curb at Jill's house without messing up the tires! It wasn't exactly parallel parking since there wasn't anyone else parked there except me. But at least I didn't hit the curb. Oh—here's the key."

"Who all came? The regular crew?"

"Pretty much. Jill, of course—and her parents were home the whole time— and Megan and Beth and Anna and Mandy. And Billy Weston stopped by for a minute to give Megan something and introduce us to his cousin who's here visiting this weekend. It was pretty much a spectacularly predictable evening."

"Completely predictable? No change in plans?" Melanie's dad's questions and the tone of his voice were beginning to make her a little nervous. "You didn't go anywhere else in the car, Melanie? Say, over to the Myers Park area? More specifically, to Randall Boulevard? Even more specifically, to your favorite pizza place at the corner of Randall and Third?"

Melanie's face fell as she realized what was happening. Somehow her dad knew she had left Jill's and gone out to get food for the group. But how? The silence was filling the room while she tried to figure out what was happening. She wished the newscaster on the TV would say something amazingly interesting to distract her dad. It was obvious her dad knew exactly where she had gone and that it wouldn't do any good to deny it.

"Yes, I did leave Jill's, but just for a minute. We called ahead to Antonio's for pizza and I volunteered to go pick it up. I know I wasn't supposed to, but Mandy had something she wanted to tell me about so she rode with me. We were only gone for a few minutes. Am I in trouble?"

"Well, you tell me. Did you do something you had agreed not to do?"

"Yes."

"Anything else? What about using the cell phone while you were driving?"

Melanie looked shocked. What was going on here? How did her dad know everything she did?

"We did use the phone—well, not me, but Mandy. She called back to Jill's to see what people wanted to drink. We forgot to ask."

Melanie didn't even wait for her dad to respond—"Dad, I'm sorry I drove somewhere else without letting you know first. But you have to tell me— how did you know I did? And how did you know the phone was used? This is creepy!"

Melanie's dad smiled a bit for the first time. "Well, I could tell you it was my fatherly instincts, but you might not believe me. So I'll tell you the truth: GPS."

"What's GPS?"

"Basically, it's a satellite tracking system. I had little devices installed on both our cars that deliver a signal to a Web site I can access and get the location of our cars at any time. They're sold as theft deterrents—so if your car is stolen the police can go right to it. While I was working on the computer

earlier tonight I just checked in at the Web site and discovered that my car wasn't at Jill's—that it was near Antonio's in Myers Park. Impressed?"

"For sure."

"My cell phone has the same GPS system installed. Since your phone's battery was dead I gave you mine to use in case of an emergency. And when I discovered it was being used in the same location as the car, well . . . I may be old and slow, sweetie, but I've still a got a few tricks up my sleeve. Like it or not, I'm with you wherever you go."

"Wow—I had no idea."

N THE LAST CHAPTER I wrote about explorers like Columbus and Magellan who lived half a millennium ago. But I did so without mentioning what admiration and wonder I have for them and their fellow conquerors of the unknown. While the consensus in their day was that the world was round, not flat, it's still hard for me to imagine what it must have taken for Columbus to set out in the *Niña*, the *Pinta*, and the *Santa Maria*, three creaky, leaky vessels by today's standards, on a September day in 1492.

They left Palos, Spain, on August 3 and sailed to Spain's Canary Islands off the northwest coast of Africa, a routine and familiar trip that could be made, if needed, in sight of land the whole way. There they made repairs and restocked the ships and left for worlds unknown on September 6, turning their backs on land and facing nothing but water.

I sometimes have that feeling when I turn my back on the California coast and point the bow of my fishing boat due west toward Asia. Saltwater fishing has been a passion of mine for years, yet there is still something seriously intimidating about the vastness of the Pacific Ocean. While the Atlantic Ocean Columbus faced is not nearly as large as the Pacific, once you stand on the deck of a boat in any ocean and turn in a circle and see nothing but water, it's an unnerving feeling.

Fortunately, when I leave my home port to go fishing in the Pacific I take with me none of the anxiety ship captains had five hundred years ago. Why? Because my boat is equipped with the modern miracle of GPS—the

Global Positioning System. Regardless how far I purposely go in my boat, or am accidentally carried by wind or currents when the motors are off, my GPS knows exactly where I am and how to get home. Columbus and his mariner kin were guided by stars in the sky, and I am guided by heavenly bodies as well. But they're not stars—they're satellites! Some two dozen man-made satellites are now in place, continually transmitting signals to earth picked up by all manner of GPS receivers. The receivers, by way of some fancy math I don't profess to understand, integrate the signals from three or four satellites (a process called trilateration) and compute your exact location on earth—whether stationary or moving.

Many cell phones are now equipped with GPS capability (think of the search and rescue benefits), as well as all manner of other devices for ships and boats, airplanes, cars, bicycles, the visually impaired, survey-ors, police, firefighters, emergency rescue personnel, heavy construction equipment, farm equipment—the list goes on and on. I understand many farmers with hundreds or thousands of acres to plow and plant now have tractors guided by computers and GPS systems resulting in perfectly aligned fields. In 2007 the burgeoning sport of NASCAR began using GPS to instantly re-create crashes using 3-D animations of car positions based on GPS reckoning.

The "All-Seeing Eye"

The all-encompassing ability of the Global Positioning System brings to mind the idea of the "all-seeing eye of God." That symbol has been found in numerous cultures—an eyeball representing God's ability to observe all of mankind's activity. Sometime in the seventeenth or eighteenth century, the eye was enclosed in a triangle, giving it a Christian Trini-tarian frame of reference. In 1782 this "Eye of Providence" was adopted as part of the reverse-side image of the Great Seal of the United States, appearing above an unfinished pyramid with thirteen steps representing the thirteen original colonies. We are most familiar with that side of the Great Seal because it appears on the backside of our one-dollar bills.

For some, the idea of a global satellite system tracking everyone's movements is a scary thought—and rightfully so. Any beneficial tech-nology can be misused by the wrong hands. And the idea of a God who is tracking our lives with His "all-seeing eye" is likewise a scary thought to a lot of people. But in this chapter I am going to say that nothing could be more comforting for the person who is on a journey through life than knowing God is ever-present with us.

Think of the comfort of having a GPS-equipped cell phone. If you find yourself lost or stranded and don't know where you are, the GPS system does. It never loses track of you. And what if you are journeying through life and find yourself lost or stranded (not to mention confused, despairing, seeking direction, or stuck), how comforting is it to know that God is with you—that He never loses track of you.

In the spring of 1905, Civilla Martin and her husband were traveling through Elmira, New York, where they became acquainted with a Mr. and Mrs. Doolittle. Here's how Mrs. Martin described a conversation that ensued between them:

> Mrs. Doolittle had been bedridden for nigh twenty years. Her husband was an incurable cripple who had to propel himself to and from his business in a wheel chair. Despite their afflictions, they lived happy Christian lives, bringing inspiration and comfort to all who knew them. One day while we were visiting with the Doolittles, my husband commented on their bright hopefulness and asked them for the secret of it. Mrs. Doolittle's reply was simple. "His eye is on the sparrow, and I know He watches me." The beauty of this simple expression of boundless faith gripped the hearts and fired the imagination of Dr. Martin and me. The hymn "His Eye Is on the Sparrow" was the outcome of that experience.
>
> (quote from Wikipedia; no original source cited)

At the height of Billy Graham's evangelistic crusade movement, almost everyone in America knew the hymn Civilla Martin wrote after meeting the Doolittles. No one who ever saw or heard Ethel Waters sing it would ever forget it:

"Why should I feel discouraged,
Why should the shadows come,

Why should my heart be lonely,
And long for heaven and home,
When Jesus is my portion?
My constant friend is He:
His eye is on the sparrow,
And I know He watches me;
His eye is on the sparrow,
And I know He watches me."

Even modern pop singers like Jessica Simpson have covered this song because of the timeless and universal appeal of its theme: if God has His eye on the sparrows He created, how much more does He have His eye on me, one who is created in His image?

The Everywhere-Present God

The theme of this song draws, of course, on the words of Jesus in Matthew 6:26 and 10:29–31, about how God values and cares for us far more than He does the sparrows for whom He also cares and provides. And Jesus was simply echoing a well-established Old Testament teaching that God is everywhere—that is, He is omnipresent.

Often the idea of God's immediacy was invoked when speaking of God's enemies—it was impossible for them to hide from God:

"Am I only a God nearby," declares the LORD, "and not a God far away? Can anyone hide in secret places so that I cannot see him?" declares the LORD. "Do not I fill heaven and earth?" declares the LORD. (Jeremiah 23:23–24; see also Amos 9:2–4)

But King David talked about God's omnipresence and omniscience (all-knowingness) in the way I'm thinking of in this chapter—in a positive way. See if you don't agree:

Where can I go from your Spirit? Where can I flee from your presence? If I go up to the heavens, you are there; if I make my bed in the depths, you are there. If I rise on the wings of the dawn, if I settle on the far side of the sea, even there your hand will guide me, your right hand will hold me fast. If I say, "Surely the darkness will hide me and the light become night around me," even the darkness will not be dark to you; the night will shine like the day, for darkness is as light to you. (Psalm 139:7–12)

David used a figure of speech common in the Hebrew language and culture: merism—citing opposites to cover the two extremes and everything in between as well. If he goes to the heavens or the depths of the sea, God is in both places and everywhere in between. If he rises on the wings of the dawn (east) and goes to the far side of the (Mediterranean) sea (west), God is in both places and everywhere in between. If he is in the darkness, God is there; if he is in the light, God is there as well—and in every shade of gray in between. David took great comfort in knowing there was nowhere he would or could go on his journey through life to escape the "all-seeing eye of God."

But there is more to this idea of God's omnipresence than just the fact He sees us wherever we are. That idea conjures up the notion God is in heaven with divinely powered binoculars peering down and keeping an eye on us. But God doesn't know where we are only because He *sees* us. He knows where we are because He is *with* us.

If I am at the beach with my children (if they were still young), it would be one thing for me to ensure their safety by sitting fifty yards back up on the beach while keeping an eye on them as they played at the water's edge. From that distance, yes, I can see them. But I don't know what they're saying or thinking or feeling. Are they fearful of the water? Did one get sand in an eye? At what are they laughing? Why are they fussing? Only when I get up from where I am and go where they are can I be in the moment with them and know the answers to those questions and provide what help I can should they need me. And that's what God does for us.

Here's the image this idea of God's presence brings to my mind: Consider yourself in the depths of a pitch-black cave where you cannot, as they say, even see your hand in front of your face. Then imagine your spouse, or someone you know well, standing face-to-face with you in the dark. But I don't mean just face-to-face—I mean nose-to-nose; as close as the two of you could be without actually touching noses. Remember—it's pitch black, so you wouldn't see this person standing there even if your eyes were open. Of course, you might hear them breathing or feel their breath on your face. But imagine that you could neither see, nor hear, nor smell, nor feel that person standing less than a hair's breadth from your face.

Then imagine someone flipped a switch and the lights came on. There you are, standing eye-to-eye, nose-to-nose, and chin-to-chin with another person whom just a moment before you had no way of knowing was there. Don't move! Imagine standing there for a few minutes, getting used to the experience of living with another person "in your face."

That's a poor example of what it means for God to be omnipresent; for Him to be immediately with you—nothing between Him and you. Every moment of every day, God is that close to you. Indeed, He is closer since He lives within. But from the perspective of human beings, our easiest frame of reference, God is in your face every second of your life. He knows what you need, what you think, how you feel, what you desire, your every longing and dream, where you hurt, and what you wish you had and hadn't done. When you need Him, He is just an eyelash away from touching you.

The passage in the Bible that best expresses God's closeness to you and to me is found in Acts 17. The apostle Paul was speaking to an audience of Greek intellectuals in Athens, men who seemed to pride themselves on not being able to know God. They "spent their time doing nothing but talking about and listening to the latest ideas" (v. 21). Paul delivered a long sermon to them about God's "knowability" and approachableness, which could be summarized with these words:

> God did this so that men would seek him and perhaps reach out for him and find him, though he is not far from each one of us. "For in him we live and move and have our being." As some of your own poets have said, "We are his offspring." (vv. 27–28)

"We live and move and have our being." It is as if Paul is saying God is the atmosphere in which we live and breathe—that mixture of mostly nitrogen and oxygen that sustains us moment by moment in our physical lives. We can't touch it or see it or taste it or smell it—but it is there. And without it, we would perish in three or four minutes. God is like that to us, Paul writes. He surrounds us with His presence. Where we go, He goes. In fact, where we go He is already there because He is everywhere. We live and move and have our being in Him.

The God Who Works with You

I began this chapter talking about the technological marvel of GPS—a system that tracks and guides things in motion. I hope the reason why—and the reason for introducing the omnipresence of God—is evident. You and I are people in motion, people on a journey through life. It is fundamentally important for us to know and remember we do not travel alone. If you are a follower of Jesus Christ, God is imminently and intimately interested in your journey. Indeed, Christ died for the purpose of ensuring you success in your journey and its completion.

There is a passage of Scripture in the book of Mark I rarely hear discussed. But I think it is one of the most endearing in all the Bible when it comes to illustrating God's interest in your journey and mine. The setting is just after Jesus' ascension into heaven following His resurrection. The Great Commission (see Matt. 28:19–20) had been delivered and it was now time for the disciples to begin their own personal journey as stewards of the responsibility given them: to start in Jerusalem and go to the ends of the earth with the gospel (see Acts 1:8).

The last verse in the book of Mark contains the thought I find so comforting on those days when my own journey gets to be a challenge: "Then the disciples went out and preached everywhere, *and the Lord worked with them* and confirmed his word by the signs that accompanied it" (Mark 16:20; emphasis added). Three words in the Greek language—*tou kuriou sunergountos* (literally, "the Lord helping in the work")—make all the difference.

How would you like to be one of a group of twelve whose job it is to change the world—by yourselves? In a day when there were no cars, no telecommunications, no printing presses—no GPS!—the twelve disciples of Christ (the original eleven plus Matthias, Judas's replacement) were given a seemingly impossible job: make disciples of all the nations and baptize them in the name of the Father, Son, and Holy Spirit. They had no resources at all except the one most important: Jesus working with them by the indwelling presence of His Spirit (see Gal. 2:20).

It will not do for us to think Jesus worked only with the original group He sent into the world. You and I are the spiritual descendants of that initial group and stewards of the same responsibility to disciple the nations for Christ. Indeed, as followers of Jesus, our lives, regardless our vocations and avocations, are given over to a journey of obedience to Him. But it is not a journey we undertake alone any more than the Twelve did. It is a journey in which Jesus "helps in the work."

There are undoubtedly days in your journey—as there are in mine—when the things God has called you to do look planet-sized and the obstacles loom like the edges of a dark, untouched continent on the horizon. Your journey may entail living in a marriage that is assailing the very vow you took to remain until death do you part. Or it may be you are being tested by an illness or some other physical challenge yielding to no human solution. Perhaps you are facing your senior years with very little money or family to depend on. Maybe your soul is weary from how your journey has reminded you more of a maze than a miracle lately.

I can only tell you what Mark told his readers—Jesus is helping you in your work. His is the face in the dark you cannot see but whom the Bible tells you is there. His is the face you see when the light of inspiration and revelation dawns in your heart and you remember you are not alone on your journey. Jesus is where you have been. Jesus is where you are. And Jesus is where you are going. And if the work you are doing is work He has given, then He is sharing in that work. You are neither traveling, nor working, alone.

A few years ago Donna and I traveled to a little village in Mexico, on the coast of the Sea of Cortez, called La Paz. While walking the streets one day we came across a shop specializing in scuba-diving excursions. Ever since our first dive together on our honeymoon we have watched for further opportunities to dive.

When we talked to the proprietor about his excursions, he was most enthusiastic about diving at El Bajo, an underwater mountain about ten miles off the coast, the top of which comes within about forty-five feet of the surface. He told us it was a place where beautiful fish congregate in abundance, but the main reason people go there is for the hammerheads.

Sharks? Then he showed us a picture taken on a recent dive and yes, he meant sharks, schools of huge eerie predators. I was sold. But selling the idea to Donna was another matter. After a lot more discussion with the proprietor and lots more questions, Donna finally agreed to go. As it turned out, the dive was everything and more than the man said—just like the pages of *National Geographic* magazine. It was spectacular and completely safe.

I've often thought about how close we came to missing an incredible experience. Donna was right to get all the needed information, but once it was obvious that there was nothing to fear it would have been a shame to let fear keep us from such a beautiful and educational event.

When God gives you an opportunity don't let fear keep you from taking it. Remember Jesus' words to His disciples when they were on the Sea of Galilee in the midst of a storm: "You of little faith, why are you so afraid?" (Matt. 8:26). The opposite of faith is not doubt—it is fear!

GPS: God's Positioning System

- It costs the United States Air Force around $750 million per year to monitor and maintain the GPS satellites (GPS Overview from the NAVSTAR Joint Program Office, accessed Dec. 15, 2006). All it costs you to be accompanied and guided by God is your faith.

- GPS uses three satellites to pinpoint your position. Between God the Father, God the Son, and God the Spirit, you are continually being ministered to by God.

- GPS receivers track a fourth satellite to correct the internal clock in the receiver. Our internal spiritual receptors are not perfect and may need occasional correcting or adjusting. Don't be afraid to verify God's direction with a trusted source who is mature in discerning God's guidance.

- Varying atmospheric conditions can hamper the transmission of signals between the GPS satellites and the receiver on earth. Be aware of negative conditions in the atmosphere of your life that might hinder God's communication with you.

- GPS signals are not often jammed, but it can happen. If you have forgotten that communication from God can be "jammed," reread the account in Genesis 3:1–7—and live on your guard.

- Clocks in GPS satellites run faster twenty-three thousand miles above the earth because of the reduced gravitational pull and the speed at which they travel (http://en.wikipedia.org/wiki/Gps). (Before being launched, they're set to run a tad slower so when they speed up in heaven they'll be on time.) Did you know God's "clock" is always ahead of yours? What you see today God has seen for all eternity. Your needs are never a surprise to Him. Your journey will never take you to a place He has not been ahead of you.

Wherever you are in your journey—starting, stumbling, or stepping out—if you are a believer in Jesus Christ you do not walk alone.

*Our challenge is to
learn to hear God's voice
as we travel.*

Signs along the Way

The LORD came and stood there, calling as at the
other times, "Samuel! Samuel!" Then Samuel said,
"Speak, for your servant is listening."

—1 Samuel 3:10

When John Sanders got home, his wife, Millie, was already in bed, reading a book. She put her bookmark in and closed the book on her lap when John walked into the bedroom.

"How's your dad?" she asked. She was trying to read John's face but couldn't find the right word to describe how he looked. Thoughtful? Relaxed? Pensive? Maybe satisfied?

"Oh, he's doing alright, I guess," John said. "He continues to amaze me. I would think that since Mom died, living alone, he'd be lonely or discouraged. But he seems healthy and satisfied. I know his faith in the Lord is a large part of it. I just hope I'm that secure when I'm his age."

"What did you all talk about?"

John didn't answer immediately. He was sitting on the side of the bed taking off his shoes and socks. Millie's question caused him to pause with his first sock halfway off.

"Well, you know, I don't know if I can really say. And it's funny you ask because I was thinking about that on the way home."

"Thinking about what?" Millie asked. This must be a clue to what she saw on John's face.

"Driving home I was thinking about the way I spend time with Dad

*now compared to how we spent time at different periods in our relation-
ship. I mean, I can go over to his house now and just hang out for a couple
of hours with him and feel completely satisfied even though I can't really
identify any one thing we talked about or did together. It's like just being
together, in the same room, is enough. I feel like we're communicating stuff
to each other even though we might be watching a ball game or just staring
into the fireplace, sipping hot chocolate. You know what I mean?" John had
been staring at the sock in his hand while he said everything but the last
sentence—which he spoke after turning to look at Millie.*

"I think so," Millie replied. "It sounds nice."

*With that affirmation John turned further around on the bed so he could
face Millie, and continued:*

*"Here's what occurred to me. Children use their parents for one thing—
to get stuff. Right? I mean, our kids used us to meet their every waking need
and I'm sure I did that with my mom and dad when I was little. And it's
okay—that's what little kids are supposed to do. They need things and nat-
urally turn to their parents to provide them. When we're little, the essence
of what we ask for is 'stuff.'*

*"But when we get a little older—like grammar school age—we ask our
parents for help. You know, help with homework, help putting a bicycle
together, help learning to hit a baseball or make a cake. But then when
we're in high school we stop asking for things and help and ask for space.
We're torn between wanting our parents there and not wanting them there.
So we ask for—or demand, I guess—space.*

*"Then we get married and have kids of our own and suddenly decide
our parents weren't as dumb as we thought and we start asking for help
again. Only this time it's more like advice. Instead of wanting what they
have, like we did when we were little, we start wanting what they know. Big
difference."*

*Millie was listening quietly, not wanting to interrupt something coming
out of a deep place in John.*

*"And then we get where Dad and I were tonight. I don't need any 'things'
from him, and my need for his help and advice are only occasional. At this
point, it's like I just need him. I just need to be in the same place as him to
watch him and listen to him and soak up everything I can. I feel like I'm*

finally wise enough to recognize that it's less about what I can get from Dad than it is about just getting him. All the things we've disagreed about over the years are so not the issue any longer. Since Mom died I see more clearly that I'm not going to have him forever and I need to soak up as much of him as I can."

Knowing John would be embarrassed if she didn't respond, Millie jumped in. "That must have been some drive home. You figured all that out in fifteen minutes?"

"Hey—I'm not as dumb as I look," John laughed, finishing his first sock and turning to the second.

⌒

WHEN IT CAME TO BURYING the thousands of Union and Confederate soldiers who lay dead on the battlefield of Gettysburg, Pennsylvania, the governor of the state commissioned a local attorney, David Wills, to establish a cemetery. Wills did so and planned a dedication ceremony for the Gettysburg cemetery. On November 2, 1863, he sent a handwritten letter to "His Excellency, A. Lincoln, President U.S." inviting him to "formally set apart these grounds to their sacred use by a few appropriate remarks" on November 19.

The battle was fought in early July. Why such a long delay for the dedication ceremony? It wasn't only because of the enormity of the task or the inevitable bureaucratic red tape that no doubt slowed the process. Indeed, Wills had planned for the dedication to be held on September 23, nearly two months prior to when it finally took place. The primary reason for the delay appears to have been a request by the keynote speaker, Edward Everett, to push back the date.

Edward Everett served the United States as secretary of state, both a senator and member of the U.S. House of Representatives, a foreign minister to Britain, America's first PhD, governor of Massachusetts, and president of Harvard University. In addition, he was widely considered to be one of, if not *the,* greatest orators in America. But when Everett was contacted about delivering the dedicatory speech, he replied that he would be unable to compose an appropriate address by September 23 and asked that the ceremony be moved back. Wills and his committee agreed and pushed the date back to November 19.

Comparing the dates of the invitations it's obvious the addition of President Lincoln to the ceremony was an afterthought. But, as so often happens in life, what was originally an afterthought became that which history remembers best.

For two hours Edward Everett spoke 13,607 words to a crowd estimated at fifteen thousand—a speech the size of a small book. To give you an idea of what the standing audience listened to for two hours, here are the opening and final sentences that America's greatest orator spoke that day:

Opening:

Standing beneath this serene sky, overlooking these broad fields now reposing from the labors of the waning year, the mighty Alleghenies dimly towering before us, the graves of our brethren beneath our feet, it is with hesitation that I raise my poor voice to break the eloquent silence of God and Nature. But the duty to which you have called me must be performed;—grant me, I pray you, your indulgence and your sympathy.

Closing:

But they, I am sure, will join us in saying, as we bid farewell to the dust of these martyr-heroes, that wheresoever throughout the civilized world the accounts of this great warfare are read, and down to the latest period of recorded time, in the glorious annals of our common country, there will be no brighter page than that which relates the Battles of Gettysburg.

After Everett's two-hour talk President Lincoln spoke, taking two minutes to say approximately 250 words. (Scholars differ on the exact wording of the original.) Here is the version of Lincoln's Gettysburg Address that is inscribed on the walls of the Lincoln Memorial in Washington, D.C. Compare this with the samples from Everett you just read:

Four score and seven years ago our fathers brought forth on this continent a new nation, conceived in liberty, and dedicated to the proposition that all men are created equal.

Now we are engaged in a great civil war, testing whether that nation, or any nation so conceived and so dedicated, can long endure. We are met on a great battlefield of that war. We have come to dedicate a portion of that field as a final resting-place for those who here gave their lives that this nation might live. It is altogether fitting and proper that we should do this.

But, in a larger sense, we can not dedicate . . . we can not consecrate . . . we can not hallow . . . this ground. The brave men, living and dead, who struggled here, have consecrated it far above our poor power to add or detract. The world will little note nor long remember what we say here, but it can never forget what they did here. It is for us the living, rather, to be dedicated here to the unfinished work which they who fought here have thus far so nobly advanced. It is rather for us to be here dedicated to the great task remaining before us . . . that from these honored dead we take increased devotion to that cause for which they gave the last full measure of devotion; that we here highly resolve that these dead shall not have died in vain; that this nation, under God, shall have a new birth of freedom; and that government of the people, by the people, for the people, shall not perish from the earth.

Are you surprised at which speech history has enshrined as one of the most moving in history?

The difference in their speeches was not lost on Everett. The day after the dedication ceremony at Gettysburg he wrote Lincoln a note saying, "I should be glad, if I could flatter myself that I came as near the central idea of the occasion in two hours, as you did in two minutes." It's interesting that one of the five remaining copies of the Gettysburg Address is one given to Everett by Lincoln. I don't know whether Everett requested it or Lincoln sent it unsolicited. Either way, Everett would have done well to take a lesson in brevity from the Speaker-in-Chief.

Learning to Talk to God

I gave the background on Lincoln's Gettysburg Address to set the stage for talking about prayer as part of our journey. Reflecting on the power of Lincoln's carefully chosen words makes me wonder whether he used another short speech—a prayer, actually—as his inspiration—one even shorter and more famous than his own: the prayer Jesus taught His disciples to pray. In only seventy-three words (in the original Greek text) Jesus created a prayer that is the model of brevity and the epitome of meaning.

Jesus' disciples had apparently been used to hearing religious leaders, both Jewish and pagan, pray long, profound prayers designed to impress hearers human and divine (like the opening and closing of Edward Everett's oration at Gettysburg) (see Matthew 6:5, 7; Mark 12:40). The disciples apparently heard Jesus pray profoundly different prayers. There was something about His prayers that struck them as being more like communication than oration. And they wanted to know how to pray like He did, and like John the Baptist (see Luke 11:1). Everything these two cousins did, Jesus and John, was different from the status quo—even the way they communed with God.

I believe I have followed a path similar to many about whom I have read when it comes to prayer. When I was a much younger Christian my prayers were all about asking God for this, that, and the other. I learned to make prayer lists and keep track of the answers I received and those I didn't. And I spent lots of introspective time analyzing my confessional life to see if there was a sin or blemish that might be preventing God from answering my prayers.

Today, I think differently. Note—I didn't say I *pray* altogether differently. I still go to my heavenly Father when I need this, that, or the other. He's my Abba Father and I'm His child, and I believe He wants me to come to Him when I have needs. I still keep track of prayers I pray for people, events, ministry, my family, and our world. I still keep up with prayers answered and prayers not. And I definitely still pay attention to my confessional life. I haven't been deceived into thinking I can be careless about sin and not have it affect my relationship with God.

But as I have pursued my own journey in life—as I have tried to find the walking shoes that fit me—I have begun to think more simply, more basically, about prayer. For instance, I try to listen at least as much, if not more so, than I speak. If I spend a half hour in prayer I will often spend a good portion of it in meditative prayer, or listening prayer, trying to be still before the Lord. As a younger Christian I would have worn myself out verbally communicating my petitions (and grievances).

It's a growing understanding of Jesus' model prayer that has helped me mature in my prayer life. And not surprisingly, I found a parallel in something attributed to former president Woodrow Wilson. He is reported to have once said, "If I am to speak ten minutes, I need a week for preparation; if fifteen minutes, three days; if half an hour, two days; if an hour, I am ready now."

Did you get his point? The shorter the amount of time he was to speak, the longer he needed to prepare for it. (Compare that to Edward Everett's opposite strategy: he spoke two hours and took two months to prepare.) Anyone who has ever written or spoken with a word count or time restraint knows it is much harder to say a little than it is to say a lot. (For instance, try to summarize your entire life in a paragraph of exactly fifty words.)

I have found I think more about spending time with God than I used to. That is, I prepare longer and say less. I think about the principles Jesus set forth in His model prayer so when I do begin to pray my words are more focused and, hopefully, in line with God's will.

Recognize God as Father

For some reason, the version of Jesus' model prayer in Matthew became the one made standard in post-Reformation Protestant liturgies and services—the one that begins, "Our Father . . ." (Matt. 6:9)—as opposed to Luke's version which begins without the possessive pronoun: "Father . . ." (Luke 11:2). I daresay that everyone who can say the Lord's Prayer from memory begins by saying, "Our Father . . ."

But there's something appealing to me about beginning my prayers with just, "Father." If I am in a family gathering with my siblings and children, no one calls my father, Robert H. Schuller "Our dad" when addressing him. We just call him "Dad." Yes, he is "our father and grand-father," but he is also father to each of us individually. If he was nobody else's father in the world, he would still be mine.

And the same is true of God. My God is also Father to hundreds of millions of other Christian believers around the world, so there is good reason to address Him as "Our Father." I find that particularly appropriate when I am leading a group in prayer—when I am speaking to God not only for myself but for others. But when I am communing with God alone, calling Him "Father" reminds me that He is everything for me I could want a father to be.

In terms of my personal journey, I view God the same way I do my earthly father. My siblings and I have all walked unique, individual paths in life, and our parents were there to encourage and provide for us individually. And I know no one else in this world is called to walk the path I am and God is personally committed to helping me find, and succeed in, that path. *I really believe that!*

Do you? Do you believe your Father God is *for you*? That He is on your team, coaching you and counseling you to help you find your shoes and wear them into the future? When you stop to commune with God in prayer, do you address Him as an institutional Father or as your personal Father? Jesus referred to God as Abba ("Papa" in the original Aramaic, a term of personal endearment; see Mark 14:36) when He was in the midst of the greatest crisis of His life. And that's what I am learning to do as well.

Praying for God's Will to Be Done

I love what the late Ruth Bell Graham, wife of Billy Graham, said about her prayer life: "I am so glad God did not listen to my foolish demands in my younger years. I would have married the wrong guy fifteen times." Who among us, looking back, cannot see some things we have asked God for we are glad He did *not* give us?

The first request Jesus taught His disciples to ask for is perhaps the most important of all: "[May] your kingdom come, your will be done, on earth as it is in heaven" (Matt. 6:10). In the final analysis, all will be well if God's will is done. Yet often our prayers are focused on our will instead of God's. The heart of this request is, "God is God and we're not." When we pray, "Your kingdom come, your will be done," we're saying, "Father, I submit to You. Whatever Your will is, I am prepared to do it."

When we request that God's will be done, we are admitting and agreeing His will is better than anything we could come up with. If we didn't believe that, why would we pray it? When we pray the Lord's Prayer in church on Sunday morning and then complain about something His will allows to happen Sunday afternoon, it makes our prayer look insincere at best and hypocritical at worst.

In terms of prayer for my personal journey I feel complete freedom to share my dreams and desires with God. But I always, always try to remember to say, "But Father, in the end, I want Your kingdom to come and Your will to be done."

Don't Worry

If you were listening to popular music in the late 1980s (or the "oldies" stations since then), you remember the song by jazz composer Bobby McFerrin, "Don't Worry, Be Happy." It reached number one on the Billboard Hot 100 chart and stayed there for two weeks in 1988 and won the Grammy for Best Song in 1989. It obviously hit a nerve with a lot of people.

What you may not know is that McFerrin got the inspiration for his catchy, a cappella tune from a Hindu spiritual master named Meher Baba. McFerrin wasn't a Hindu himself—he just borrowed the "don't worry, be happy" phrase from Baba who used it as a mantra of sorts. It had a fatalistic flavor to it, drawing on the Hindu eternally cyclical view of life where one tries to improve his lot in life each time he is re-created and comes back for another cycle. In other words, "do the best you can and then let things work themselves out."

Many people today live by that philosophy—even many Christians. They believe "you can't fight city hall"—whatever will be, will be. But that is not the impression Jesus gave His disciples. He told them to ask their heavenly Father to meet their needs: "Give us today our daily bread" (Matt. 6:11). In other words, asking can make the difference between having daily bread or not.

This simple request reminds me of Abraham Lincoln's Gettysburg Address—packing a world of sentiment and emotion and meaning into the fewest possible words. "Bread" doesn't mean bread only. It's a metonymy, a figure of speech in which one word is substituted for many: "Father, give me today the food I need and all else my journey requires." And since Jesus told the disciples the Father knows what they need before they ask (see Matt. 6:8), our request to God is more an affirmation: "Father, You know these needs I have. I come not to tell You but to trust You; not to inform You but to inspire myself."

You and I will have many needs on our journey, needs of which our Father in heaven is already well aware. When we meet with Him in prayer our time is equally well spent silently rehearsing His past faithfulness in addition to thanking Him ahead of time for meeting our new needs.

Keep Us from Evil

The traditional version of the Lord's Prayer most of us learned is based on the King James Version of the Bible: "deliver us from evil" (Matt. 6:13). But most modern English translations of the Bible have personalized that request based on a better understanding of the original Greek language: "deliver us from the evil one." There are two requests in verse 13 that are two sides of the same coin: keep us from temptation and protect us from Satan.

Satan loves nothing better than to find our weaknesses, our hot buttons, and exploit them. He tempts us to heal our wounds with all sorts of ineffective balms—sex, drink, food, ambition, wealth, power, prestige . . . the list goes on. But it is only when we reaffirm who we are in Christ—a child of the God who has healed our wounds by Christ's wounds (see Isa. 53:5)—that we are protected from the evil one. (It goes without saying here that unforgiveness is like extending an engraved invitation to Satan to tempt us with bitterness and resentment. Don't fail to forgive as you are forgiven [see Matt. 6:12].)

When I pray about my journey I rehearse before God who I am in Christ and in doing so clothe myself with the only armor able to protect me from the attacks of my enemy (see Eph. 6:10–18). Alone, I am fair game for him. In Christ, my journey cannot be stopped.

Establish a Foundation

Some modern Bible versions, based on a discrepancy in the Greek text of Matthew, leave out what has to be the perfect conclusion to Jesus' model prayer: "For Yours is the kingdom and the power and the glory forever. Amen" (Matt. 6:13 NKJV). Even if that statement is not part of Jesus' original words to His disciples, it is so biblical it forms a solid foundation for how to pray about our journey.

If our journey is about anyone else's kingdom, power, and glory than God's, then we shouldn't expect His blessing along the way. Conversely, if our journey is all about God's kingdom, power, and glory then we have every reason to expect God to bless it and make it successful. If you want a way to implement this idea in your journey prayers, tell God something like this after you've prayed for His will to be done, for your needs to be met, and for forgiveness and protection: "Father, please reveal to me any way I am usurping Your right to rule, Your power, or Your glory. I'm listening—please tell me."

If you pray that prayer you will be told if you are casting an inappropriate shadow across the landscape of God's kingdom. And if you make the adjustments God shows you, your journey will continue with His blessing. I can't think of any reason why a follower of Jesus would want to do otherwise.

If you are searching for your walking shoes, a good place to look for them is in your prayer closet. And remember, it's not about your words or your list. It's about God. The more you find Him in prayer, the more you'll find all else you seek.

Reader Note

The Web site for our television broadcast, *The Hour of Power* (www.hourofpower.org), is using technology to increase the amount of prayer being offered around the world. There is a Prayer Community on the Web site into which anyone in the world may enter. You can request prayer for yourself or offer prayers for others. You can even create a prayer journal online to track your life and ministry of prayer. It is truly becoming a community of online friends who are sharing in each others' lives through the ministry of prayer. I encourage you to visit the Prayer Community and participate. Nothing stimulates prayer in our lives like being able to pray with others.

Sources for Lincoln material if needed:

http://en.wikipedia.org/wiki/Gettysburg_Address

http://www.loc.gov/exhibits/gadd/gainvi.html

http://www.loc.gov/exhibits/gadd/gadrft.html

http://usinfo.state.gov/usa/infousa/facts/democrac/25.htm

http://www.ourdocuments.gov/doc.php?flash=true&doc=36

http://en.wikipedia.org/wiki/Edward_Everett

We need to grow up
before we grow old, and
that is what the journey
is designed to do. We have
to embrace that which
will make us grow.

Motion Is Not the Same as Progress

Brothers, I do not consider myself yet to have taken hold of it. But one thing I do: Forgetting what is behind and straining toward what is ahead, I press on toward the goal to win the prize for which God has called me heavenward in Christ Jesus.

—Philippians 3:13–14

Barry Lester was forty years old, married faithfully and happily to Susan, and father to two great kids—Barry Jr. and Sally Ann. He had a job he loved as a senior VP in a community bank and seemed to have time to stay involved in his kids' lives and with his wife. They attended a church in town in which they were relatively happy, participating in as many different ways as they could. Barry's life was busy, but not frantic. He was satisfied, but not particularly excited. He was content to the degree that he wasn't thinking of doing anything crazy, but discontent to the point that it crossed his mind occasionally.

And it bothered him that he wasn't frantic in a good sense (overwhelmed with life's possibilities); bothered that he wasn't excited instead of comfortable; bothered that he hadn't taken a risk since asking the homecoming queen for a date in college (a disaster). He stewed about this internally in his quiet moments, but had no idea what the answer was.

When it was announced at church that a new program was underway to get small groups of three to five men together for every-two-week meetings, he decided it might be a good place to air his laundry—get some feedback from some other guys. He and two friends discussed the idea, rounded up two more mutual friends, and declared themselves "a group" as part of the new men's initiative.

The church suggested some basic goals for the groups—making and deepening friendships, becoming a safe haven for seeking help or advice, growing in the discipline of prayer for one another, integrating scriptural truth into the discussions—but left it to each group to establish a format that was suitable for accomplishing those goals.

Since Barry initiated their group's formation, he took it upon himself to begin their discussion the first time they met. After greetings and pleasantries, he brought up the goals the church distributed.

"Well, guys, as a place to start, I'll throw out on the table the one particular goal on this list that intrigues me—and then let you guys respond. I am more than comfortable with Scripture and prayer, and, of course, look forward to us building even better friendships by meeting together. But it was this one—'safe haven for seeking help or advice'—that caught my attention.

"Don't panic—I'm not here to confess to anything dastardly. Everything with Susan, the kids, and work, is great. In fact, that may be part of the problem. I've sort of been getting the feeling the last couple of years that my life is on cruise control; that I, and our family, have a great routine in place . . . we're on a peaceful, prosperous journey to somewhere—but I don't know where. I feel like we're in motion, but I'm not sure how to define the progress we're making—or whether we're making any at all.

"Or maybe it's just my progress; my growth. I know we're making progress with the kids, bringing them along through adolescence and all. And Susan and I are making progress, I guess, as a couple in raising them. But it's me, as an individual, that I'm not quite sure about. I go from Monday to Monday in a steady state of activity, of motion, and I can see myself perpetuating this motion twenty or thirty years out into the future without anything particularly measurable to look back on. And to be honest, that scares me a bit."

Barry leaned back in his chair and let the room absorb the sound of his voice for a moment. When he looked up from his lap the other four guys were staring at him, but nothing was said.

"What? Was I speaking Greek there, guys?" Barry asked, smiling. "Come on—don't leave me twisting in the wind here."

Barry's friend Sonny spoke first. "Well, Bare, I guess I'm just sitting here wondering when it was you came by my house and stole my mail. I thought I was the only person I knew who felt that way—lots of motion but questionable amounts of progress. I would define my feelings this way: I'm not sure I've grown much in the last ten years. You know, you learn enough to get to a certain level in life—marriage, family, kids, business—and then it's easy to stop growing. It's easier to go with the flow, accept the status quo, than to keep pushing for the borders. When I was younger I felt like I lived with arrows in my hat—you know, doing the pioneer thing. But I haven't seen that hat for years. Except for more pounds and less hair, I'm not sure how different I am from the man I was a decade ago. And that bothers me."

After Sonny broke the ice, Fred, Wynn, and Larry set down their coffee cups and moved farther forward in their chairs. Looks like we're gonna have a discussion, Barry thought to himself.

T O BE A PLAIN, NO-NAME follower of Jesus during the 1500s and early 1600s in England was a life-threatening pursuit. Indeed, many died for traveling such a journey. Here's why:

Because of his spats with the Roman Catholic heirarchy, King Henry VIII, in the 1534 Act of Supremacy, declared himself "the only supreme head on earth of the Church of England." His son and successor, Edward VI, moved England further in the direction of Protestantism during his six-year reign. But Edward's successor, who was also Henry VIII's daughter, Mary Tudor, was a devout Catholic who restored England to Catholicism. The tables turned again when Mary's sister and successor, Elizabeth I, repealed all of Mary's Catholic policies and established herself as the head of the Church of England. When Elizabeth died in 1603, James I took the throne and insisted on being the head of both the secular (civil) and spiritual realms of England. Guess who this did not sit well with—and for good reason? The Presbyterians, also known as Puritans.

Remember, the Protestant Reformation began with Martin Luther in Germany in 1517, and a century later—during the reign of James I in England—Puritan (Reformation) theology was firmly planted among true English believers. But they had a problem: They didn't think the pope in Rome was the head of the church, nor did they believe the king or queen of England should be head of the church. They believed Christ was the head of the church.

I said earlier that these believers were no-name—neither Anglican nor Roman Catholic. But they eventually were given a name: Separatists. They chose to separate themselves from both Roman Catholicism and the Church of England and worship the Lord in house churches. They were few in number, but they were determined. They wanted more for their spiritual lives—and many of them paid dearly.

One such Separatist pastor in England was John Robinson. To escape persecution in England he advocated emigration to Europe. He and most of his congregation, in spite of amazing hardships just trying to get across the English Channel, made their way to Holland, settling in Leyden in 1609. Attracting other English who fled the persecution, they established a church and small community of faith of some three hundred souls and began to worship freely—strangers in a foreign land. Even though John Robinson was Cambridge educated, he became a student for a time at the University of Leyden. He had a hunger to grow, to know more of God's truth. He became known in Leyden as a skilled teacher and defender of the Calvinist-Puritan theology.

But many of the English émigrés soon grew discontent. They did not want to be an oddity in Holland and knew they couldn't return to England under James I. It was decided they should move again, this time to the virgin shores of America. Robinson even wrote to King James I in England asking if he would guarantee their safety and religious freedom in America. The answer was no. But they would not be dissuaded. John Robinson would remain in Leyden with part of the church while more than a hundred would leave and establish a new colony in the New World—hopefully far enough away from England's oversight to be able to worship freely.

On September 6, 1620, the *Mayflower* set sail for America, arriving there on November 11. The story of the journey and landing of those Puritan-pilgrims is for another time. But it is a metaphor for this chapter—the willingness and desire to push forward in life's faith-journey in spite of mountainous obstacles.

Another part of that metaphor is found in the life and words of John Robinson himself. The last sermon he preached to his departing flock in Holland contained these words, to which I have added my own emphases and additions for clarity:

> Brethren, we are now quickly to part from one another, and only the God of heaven knows whether I will see your face again. I charge you before God and His blessed angels that [when you get to the New World] you follow me no further than you have seen me follow the Lord Jesus Christ. *I am verily persuaded that the Lord yet has more truth to break forth from His holy Word.*
>
> I bewail the condition of the Reformed churches who will go at present no further than the instruments of their reformation [Martin Luther and John Calvin]. The Lutherans can not be drawn to go beyond what [Martin] Luther said. And the Calvinists stick fast where they were left by what the great man of God [John Calvin] said, *yet who saw not all things.* Though they [Luther and Calvin] were burning and shining lights, *they penetrated not into the whole counsel of God.* Were they now living, they would embrace further light as that which they just received.

(Reference online at: http://books.google.com/books?id=eplLzn75jikC&printsec=titlepage&vq=bewail#PPR44,M1)

Do you see what John Robinson was secure enough to tell his departing congregation? You must push forward in Christ and in the Word! Your journey is just beginning! There is a danger in getting bogged down in tradition, in what God showed us yesterday. There is infinite light to be found in the Word of God, and it will be revealed to those who seek it. The journey is in the future. There is new growth to be experienced every day. Push on! I have taken you only so far as your pastor. It is up to you to keep on growing when you arrive in the New World. Yes, God shows things to leaders, but He wants to give *you* the light that you need if you are ready to receive it.

I find Pastor Robinson's words humbling, challenging, and refreshing. He knew God was totally capable of leading his church members into deeper things than they experienced under his oversight in Holland. And he wasn't afraid to say so. He was confident and optimistic with a great sense of trust in God's leading for those who desired it. What a wonderful perspective to communicate to those about to set sail across a vast ocean to begin a new life of freedom in a free land.

Growth Requires Patience

Here's another part of Pastor Robinson's perspective I like: growth takes time. He also told those who were departing to weigh everything carefully with one another; to use one another as sounding boards about what God was saying. Because, he said, "It is not possible the Christian world should come so lately out of such thick Antichristian darkness, and that full perfection of knowledge should break forth at once." Learning and growth take time. Insights come here and there, one at a time. "Full perfection" doesn't "break forth at once."

How impatient we get. In terms of direction and counsel for our journey, we want the whole loaf every time we sit down at the table instead of drawing our nourishment from the daily bread God provides. Pastor Robinson was wise enough to know that it is God's way to reveal truth and direction as we need to know them. Think of Psalm 119:105. The truth of this verse is almost a cliché in Christian circles, but it is the truth nonetheless: "Your word is a lamp to my feet and a light for my path." A tiny oil lamp in the day that was written would illuminate a few feet ahead at best. The writer had no concept of seeing all the way down the path at once. But in our day we're not content with just a few feet. We want to see the starting line and the finish line at the same time.

I have a friend who is almost sixty years old and has been a believer since the age of twenty. During those forty years he has chronicled five specific "Eureka!" periods in his life, all of which led to years of reflection and application before the next one began. He is currently in the midst of the fifth of those "revelations" about his life and is seeking God's will for how to move forward. The specifics of his insights are not important for this discussion since they would mean little to anyone but him. But they have been vitally important to him, shaping his understanding of himself and his relationship with God.

But look how slowly they came—on average every eight years. And he is convinced there will be more as he continues following the path God is laying out before him. That's what I mean (and what John Robinson meant, I'm sure) by "full perfection" not "breaking forth at once." Anyone searching for God's path for his or her life must be willing to walk in what light God gives today, confident there will be more when it is needed.

Growth Requires Hunger

William Bradford was the second governor of the Plymouth Colony established in the New World by the Separatists. Having known John Robinson personally, Bradford's reflections on Robinson at the time of his death in Holland in 1625 give insight into this remarkable man:

> He was never satisfied in himself until he had searched any cause or argument he had to deal in thoroughly and to the bottom. And we have heard him sometimes say to his familiars that many times, both in writing and disputation, he knew he had sufficiently answered others, but many times not himself; *and was ever desirous of any light, and the more able, learned, and holy the persons were, the more he desired to confer and reason with them.*

(From the Online Library of Liberty: http://oll.libertyfund.org/Home3/ HTML.php?recordID=0063)

That kind of attitude reminds me of the words of Proverbs 2:3–5: "And if you call out for insight and cry aloud for understanding, *and if you look for it as for silver and search for it as for hidden treasure,* then you will understand the fear of the LORD and find the knowledge of God" (emphasis added).

True growth, progress, and depth in life begin with knowing God. And knowing God takes effort. Just as gold and silver require digging, so understanding the fear of the Lord and gaining the knowledge of God require digging as well. Those who want to make progress in their journey will be like John Robinson—they will find the most able, learned, and holy people they can with whom to "confer and reason."

It's important for us to separate motion from progress. They can be the same, but not always. In fact, every person I have ever talked with who was having trouble making progress in their spiritual and life journey has been a person in motion. Their problem has been (and I have experienced this problem at times in my own life), their motion was not taking them forward. What I like about John Robinson and the English Separatists is that they refused to settle for anything less than the whole enchilada, as we say in Southern California—regardless the cost. Facing enormous difficulties and obstacles, Pastor Robinson encouraged them on; encouraged them not to settle for less; encouraged them to find what their heart wanted more than anything: freedom to be who they knew God called them to be—worshipers in spirit and truth.

I can't imagine any dream beating in the heart of any follower of Jesus that should go unfulfilled. Yes, there are obstacles. But for anyone whose hunger to accomplish what God has put in his or her heart, it can be done. Even if all you can do right now is pray and learn, do that. Go to any large bookstore and look at the magazine display sections. There are specialty magazines, not to mention books, on almost every subject in the world—not to mention what's available on the Internet. Information is no longer the problem in our world. We are deluged by it! One benefit of having all this information is that it puts responsibility for the fulfillment of our dreams, the furthering of our journey, squarely on us. When we combine a hunger to know God with a hunger to get fitted for our walking shoes, we will turn motion into progress and growth in our lives.

Growth Requires Priorities

Even reading my short account of the Separatists—and how they became the "Pilgrims" of grammar school history-lesson fame—should reveal one thing: they were clear on their priorities. They were not about religion—they had that when England was Roman Catholic under Mary Tudor. Nor were they about Protestantism—they had that under Elizabeth I and James I. Their priority was worshiping God in spirit and in truth. And if that meant enduring hardships, so be it. They chose to live on the thin edge of the wedge—on the bleeding edge (literally) of their faith. And anyone today who wants to grow in their personal life and their life with God may have to do the same.

By that I don't mean you'll have to suffer as a martyr. (Nor do I mean you won't.) Rather, I mean you will need to choose your priorities in life and pursue them first above all distractions. (Choosing the best over the good and better.) Listen to what another Separatist-of-sorts, Oswald Chambers, wrote: "Joy comes from seeing the complete fulfillment of the specific purpose for which I was created and born again, not from successfully doing something of my own choosing. The joy our Lord experienced came from doing what the Father sent Him to do. And He says to us, 'As the Father has sent Me, I also send you' (John 20:21 [NKJV])."

While I believe that Isaiah's attitude toward God—"Here I am. Send me!" (Isa. 6:8)—is the starting place for finding one's purpose, I also believe our heart's desires and God's desires often overlap. We've all wrestled with the proverbial possibility of God sending us to be a "missionary in Africa" if we open ourselves to Him. But I've never met many people whom God sent to "Africa" who didn't ultimately discover that it was the perfect calling for them. Yes, God has a mission to accomplish in this world and that will entail giving out assignments. But God has also shaped us in our mother's womb and given us spiritual gifts that coincide with His purpose for our lives.

When I talk to people searching for their purpose in life, they usually talk about "needing to know" and "needing insight"—they want to find what is "best" for them in life. Knowledge, insight, finding what's best—the apostle Paul said we find those things not by pursuing *them* but by pursuing love. Did you know everything we need for ourselves in life comes as a by-product of loving God and loving others?

Here's how Paul puts it: "And this is my prayer: that your love may abound more and more in knowledge and depth of insight, so that you may be able to discern what is best and may be pure and blameless until the day of Christ, filled with the fruit of righteousness that comes through Jesus Christ—to the glory and praise of God" (Phil. 1:9–11). He doesn't pray that knowledge and insight will abound, though that's generally where we start. He prays that *love* may abound.

It was the Separatists' love for God that motivated their spiritual growth and their willingness to do whatever it took to express that love freely. In doing so, they did a small thing like helping to found a new society and culture in a New World. They decided to offer their bodies as living sacrifices, holy and pleasing to God, as a spiritual act of worship, and to refuse to be squeezed into a seventeenth-century English religious mold. In the process, they discovered God's "good, pleasing and perfect will" for their lives (see Rom. 8:28).

Is setting and sticking to priorities in life easy? No. Does it produce instant results? No. But if those priorities—especially the priority of love—line up with Scripture, will you ultimately find your journey and God's journey for you merging? I believe you will.

Growth Requires Leaving the Past Behind

There's a generally accepted axiom among successful stock traders that says, "Cut your losses and let your winners ride!" For instance, if the price of a stock falls by 20 percent (say, from ten dollars to eight), then it only has to experience a rise of 25 percent (from eight dollars back to ten) for you to break even. But, if you allow a stock to fall in price by 80 percent (say, from ten dollars to two), then that stock has to rise by *400* percent (from two dollars back to ten) for you to break even. How many times do you hear of a stock rising by 400 percent? The point is, the longer you stay with a position in stocks—or in life—that is falling or failing, the larger the recovery is needed to reverse that fall.

Yet how often we fail to cut our losses! Maybe it's a relationship or a job or a destructive habit. Because we have invested heavily in that life position we don't want to let it go. We feel as though we're cutting off a part of our identity. And we are. But often it's a part that has to go if we are to begin the process of self-discovery and fulfillment.

The Broadway star Portia Nelson wrote a book in the 1970s titled *There's a Hole in My Sidewalk: The Romance of Self-Discovery.* (If you saw the movie *Good Will Hunting,* you saw a poster on the wall of Dr. Maguire's [Robin Williams's] office showcasing this book.) In her book she included the following "Autobiography in Five Short Chapters." I've never read such a succinct presentation of how difficult the process is of learning from our mistakes and leaving the past behind and choosing a new "street," a new path, on which to walk:

There's a Hole in My Sidewalk:
Autobiography in Five Short Chapters

Chapter One
> I walk down the street.
> There is a deep hole in the sidewalk.
> I fall in.
> I am lost . . . I am helpless.
> It isn't my fault.
> It takes forever to find a way out.

Chapter Two
> I walk down the street.
> There is a deep hole in the sidewalk.
> I pretend that I don't see it.
> I fall in again.
> I can't believe I am in this same place.
> But, it isn't my fault.
> It still takes a long time to get out.

Chapter Three
> I walk down the same street.
> There is a deep hole in the sidewalk.
> I see it is there.
> I still fall in . . . it's a habit . . . but, my eyes are open.
> I know where I am.
> It is *my* fault.
> I get out immediately.

Chapter Four
> I walk down the same street.
> There is a deep hole in the sidewalk.
> I walk around it.

Chapter Five
   I walk down another street.

(*There's a Hole in My Sidewalk*, Portia Nelson, Beyond Words Publishing, Hillsboro, OR, 1994)

Sometimes we don't see the light in life until chapter two or three or even later. But better to see it and choose another street than to remain in a deep hole forever.

I don't know for sure, but the Separatists in England must have used the apostle Paul as an inspiration for leaving the past behind. First, they left England (their property, jobs, relations, and reputations) to journey to Holland. And then, after a decade or so there they left it all again. Taking only what they could pack into a few boxes and trunks, they boarded the *Mayflower* and sailed away.

Rarely will any of us be called upon to cut our physical losses so drastically. But we may well be called upon to cut our spiritual and emotional losses if we are going to grow up before we grow old. And that's what Paul did. The account of his life before meeting Christ is well documented in the New Testament (see Acts 22:3; Phil. 3:4–6). He was a rising star in the Pharisees' pantheon. He was brilliant, fearless, zealous, and relentless. And wrong. When Paul met Jesus in a blinding encounter on the road to Damascus (see Acts 9), he realized he was in a deep hole. And by the grace of God, he climbed out and began walking down another street.

If you find yourself in a "hole" of some sort at present, hemmed in by walls that will never allow you to fulfill God's plan for your life, then take Paul's words to heart: "But whatever *was* to my profit I *now* consider loss for the sake of Christ. . . . I consider them rubbish, that I may gain Christ. . . . I press on to take hold of that for which Christ Jesus took hold of me. . . . *Forgetting what is behind and straining toward what is ahead,* I press on toward the goal to win the prize for which God has called me heavenward in Christ Jesus. *All of us who are mature should take such a view of things*" (Phil. 3:7–8, 12–15; emphasis added). (Maturity also requires that we not violate God's standards or desires when cutting our losses. Obedience toward God and integrity toward self will never sanction anything but love toward others.)

Both of Oscar Pistorius's legs were amputated below the knee when he was less than a year old. In 2007, he was on track to make the South African Olympic team as a sprinter. Because he is so fast, running on his elegant carbon-fiber composite calves and feet, the International Association of Athletics Federations is having to decide whether his artificial legs give him an advantage over sprinters with natural legs. In a story in the March 2007 issue of *Wired* magazine, Pistorius is quoted as saying, "I tell people this all the time: You'll never progress if your mind is on your disability."

Don't mistake motion for progress and growth in your life. Be patient, be hungry, establish your priorities, and don't be afraid to cut your losses. The most mature people you know have had to do all four—and so will you.

There is a story about a weak old man who heard God telling him to go and push the large boulder in his yard. And the man obeyed. Day after day, month after month, year after year he would push the rock. One day Satan came to the man and asked him how far he had actually moved the rock. "Not an inch," the man replied. "I haven't moved it at all."

"You are obviously a failure," the devil said. "God never told you to push this rock. If He had, you would have moved it by now."

The man thought about what the devil said and approached God, admitting he pushed the rock for years but hadn't moved it at all.

"I never told you to move the rock," God said. "I only told you to push it. And look at how you have changed through your obedience. Whereas you were weak when you started, now you are strong and healthy. You are a different person than the man I first told to push the rock. You may not be able to move the rock, but I can. And you have exercised the kind of faith, through your efforts, that it takes for Me to act."

Was there motion from the old man's efforts? No. Was there progress? Yes. Don't mistake motion for progress in your life. They can coincide, but often they don't. If you don't see motion (progress, advancement) in your life, don't think there is not progress taking place. If you will take it up with God, as the old man did, you will learn what progress you have made.

What is a successful journey?
How do we know God
approves of our journey?
How do we define our
own success instead of adopting
someone else's?

Setting Your Direction

In everything [David] did he had great success,
because the LORD was with him.

—1 Samuel 18:14

Randy graduated from college in May and felt good about his life. His college experience had been relatively pressure-free since he already knew what he was going to do when he graduated: go home to the rugged mountains of North Georgia where he up grew and work for the family business.

His parents were outdoor types whose lives and business were intertwined in the tourist-heavy mountain town where they lived. Randy's grandfather started the business as a hardware and general store in this small mountain community. But as the mountains became a destination area for vacationers and second-home owners, Randy's father joined the business and expanded it into an outdoor gear and clothing store while retaining the charm of a century-old, one-of-a-kind, if-we-don't-have-it-you-probably-don't-need-it supply store—creaky wood floors, pot-bellied stove that burned nine months of the year (a huge iron skillet full of Georgia peanuts roasting on the top), and business (mostly) on a handshake.

But there was something Randy wanted to do before he started working full-time in the store: walk all 2,175 miles of the Appalachian Trail—from Springer Mountain in Georgia to Mount Katahdin in Maine. It had been a dream of his for years. He was an expert hiker and outdoorsman and the A.T. was the holy grail of hikes for anyone east of the Mississippi—or west, for that matter.

And he wanted to do it alone.

His parents weren't too sure about the alone part, for safety reasons, but with GPS and cell phone the idea of a solo hike was less dangerous than it used to be. So they gave their blessing, anxious for Randy to complete this outdoor rite of passage. The idea of having an A.T. thru-hiker working at the store would add extra cachet to an already-respected business.

But things didn't work out like Randy planned. Leaving Springer Mountain full of optimism he made it through Tennessee, North Carolina, Virginia, West Virginia, Maryland, and Pennsylvania—about half way. His phone calls home to his parents became more frequent, his voice sounding more dispirited. He was safe and basically healthy, but he was lonely and discouraged. Two weeks of rain left him waterlogged and miserable. He abandoned his trek and caught a flight to Atlanta where his father picked up a discouraged and embarrassed son.

"I can't believe I didn't finish," he said to his dad on the drive home. "I'm just not used to failing. I don't like the idea of telling people I hiked half the A.T."

"Well, I understand how you feel. But I wonder if perhaps you're defining failure and success too narrowly," his dad offered. He took Randy's silence as permission to continue.

"Setting out, you probably saw reaching Mount Katahdin as the sole measure of success. By that measure, not reaching it meant you failed. But I think you should consider more measures of success than just finishing the hike."

"Like what?" Randy asked.

"Well, like succeeding at having a dream bigger than most people would even contemplate. Like succeeding at accumulating a vast amount of knowledge you can pass on to others. Like succeeding in being alone with yourself for weeks on end, something many people are scared to do. Like succeeding in the discovery of new things about yourself—that you may be more of a businessman and people person than a hard-core wilderness hiker. Like succeeding in the wisdom to know when it's time to stop. Like succeeding in field-testing some of the new gear you took with you. Like succeeding in taking care of yourself in a dangerous environment. So you failed in one thing—not finishing the hike—but you succeeded in a half dozen or more other things."

Randy was listening, so his dad continued: "Success is an elusive thing,

Randy. We get things like pride and preconceptions all mixed in there and sometimes lose sight of the value of life not happening just as we planned. If I were you, I'd allow yourself room to think of this summer as a success rather than a failure. I believe you'll probably look back on this experience as a milestone of sorts in the future; a benchmark where you gained some insights you wouldn't have gained any other way."

"Maybe so," Randy said.

After a few miles of silence, Randy spoke again: "You know, all I could think about when I was cold and soaking wet was sitting by the iron stove, smelling the peanuts roasting, and teaching people how to tie rope knots and plan their next hike. Maybe that's the stuff I'm best at."

"You may have a point," his dad said as the road wound into the mountains.

W HETHER YOU ARE AWARE of it or not, you—or for sure, your children—owe a debt of gratitude to a man named Frank Epperson. In 1905, Frank was just eleven years old and, like most children his age, liked to mix soda-water powder with water to create a fizzy drink. One day Frank made himself a fizzy drink but for some reason never got around to consuming it. He left it sitting in a cup on the back porch with the stirring stick sitting in it—and it froze solid overnight. The next morning Frank discovered the cup and was able to extract the frozen soda water with a wooden stick as a handle. After licking the soda water off the stick, it didn't occur to the accidental inventor to try it again. But eighteen years later when the incident crossed his mind he began producing (and patented) the "Epsicle ice pop" in various fruit flavors. Never heard of Epsicle ice pops? Me neither. But we've all heard of the product by the name Frank's children gave it: Popsicles. Frank sold the rights to the Popsicle to a food company in 1925, but with patent in hand I'm assuming the transaction was a sweet deal for him and his family.

You know by now that I'm a fan of the serendipitous nature of this life we lead. And by serendipitous, I don't mean random or accidental—I mean unexpected, surprising, and ever changing. I mean the fact that every day is an open book with a fresh page to read. We never know what we will encounter. It could be something that changes our life completely or it could be the addition of one small piece to a puzzle we have worked on for a long time. The results could be immediate or the results might take years to realize and appreciate. For people who are in the process of finding their own walking shoes, every day on the path is a new adventure guided by a good God who loves nothing better than to surprise His children with good gifts along the way.

And Frank Epperson is a perfect example of someone who discovered a path to travel he never considered as he set out to find his own walking shoes. In fact, history is full of such stories. I'm going to give you a condensed version of a few more to whet your appetite for the theme of this chapter: the chameleon-like nature of success.

- In the early 1970s a 3M employee, Art Fry, was looking for something to mark the pages in his hymn book at choir practice—something that wouldn't fall out when he turned the pages. He remembered an adhesive a scientist at 3M came up with that hadn't been used because it was too weak. It would stick, but then it could be easily unstuck. Fry put some of Dr. Spencer Silver's adhesive on small pieces of paper and stuck them on the pages of his hymnal. Perfect! They stayed in place but they also came off easily without tearing or staining the pages of his hymn book. Your life is cluttered with the result: Post-It Notes.

- When a British bacteriologist named Alexander Fleming was researching the flu virus in 1928, he noticed a previously used petri dish in his lab with mold growing in it. Instead of being perturbed at a dish that hadn't been cleaned, he decided to investigate the strange green mold. He identified it as *penicillium notatum* and discovered it was destroying the dangerous staphylococcus bacteria in the dish. Investigating further, he concluded the mold was not stable enough to be useful, but gave it the name "penicillin" anyway. Three years later, two Oxford researchers began research that led to a more stable form of penicillin, the world's best-known antibiotic that saved countless lives in World War II. Fleming ultimately shared a Nobel Prize with the other researchers for his discovery.

- On a summer day in 1948, Swiss inventor George de Mestral returned home from walking his dog only to find his dog's coat and his own pants legs covered with burrs—those aggravating seed-pods that attach themselves to animals' fur to hitchhike to a new location. In an inspired moment he put one of the burrs under his microscope and realized the burrs had tiny hooks on their surface that snagged the threads in his pants. He realized he could create a two-part fastener—one side with hooks, the other side with loops—that might be just as useful at holding things together as buttons or zippers. When stuck together the hooks would snag the loops and—voilà!—Velcro (a combination of "velour" and "crochet") was born.

- A German physicist, Dr. Röntgen, was experimenting with cath-ode ray tubes in 1895, the same tubes that today provide images in tube-type televisions and computer monitors. In a darkened room he noticed a glow escaping a tube completely covered with black cardboard. He later discovered that those rays would pass through the human body and expose photographic film on the other side—and in 1901 he received a Nobel Prize for his discovery of X-rays.

- You have probably used cyanoacrylate before without knowing its technical name. It's what Dr. Harry Coover labeled the compound he came up with in the Kodak laboratory in 1942 when he was looking to create a clear plastic. Unfortunately, cyanoacrylate was too sticky and was put on the shelf. In 1951 Coover and an asso-ciate looked at it again, this time getting in trouble for sticking a very expensive pair of lenses together. Eventually, a lightbulb went on and in 1958 cyanoacrylate came to market—as Superglue.

I cite these examples—and there are a countless number of them in history, some well known, most not—to point out how elusive suc-cess in life is. Some of the people I've just mentioned achieved grand successes—world-changing, history-making successes—while failing at what they were attempting to accomplish. From what I know of them, inventors and scientists, followed by entrepreneurs, are probably best at managing the success-failure continuum. They understand that life is full of unexpected discoveries and results. Like the proverbial story of Thomas Edison and his "1,000" attempts at creating the ideal filament for a lightbulb—the first "999" attempts were successes because he learned what wouldn't work. By simply going through the process of eliminating them he knew he would eventually succeed at finding what did work.

The rest of us are not as good at this. When something doesn't go the way we plan, we are quick to see ourselves as the culprit. We're not smart enough, strong enough, good enough, or savvy enough to succeed. After enough false starts and the resulting negative self-talk we give ourselves, we realize the way to avoid the pain is to stop trying: the best way to stop crushing our thumb is to stop swinging the hammer. So we settle into a safe and predictable routine—and eliminate the word *succeed* from our mental lexicon.

I'd like to challenge that paradigm, that way of thinking, in this chapter, not only from a practical perspective but from a spiritual one as well.

As a child, I never won an award for academic work in school. Instead of graduating *summa cum laude*, I graduated "thank the laude." My teachers never had high hopes for me after I was in their classes. I would start each class with a bang and then somehow fizzle toward the end. I was a daydreamer who could leave the classroom mentally and not return for an hour or more. My mother would dutifully ask me after school if I had homework and I would honestly say no—because I failed to hear it announced or simply forgot about it.

I was not what anyone would call a great success in my early academic career. On the other hand, when I began to develop a vision for my life, things changed. I graduated from an excellent college, earned a master's degree in divinity from an outstanding academic seminary, and was ordained into the Christian ministry on September 21, 1980. Looking back, I realize that initial indicators for my success were not good. Fortunately, nobody told me. I guess I lacked the common sense to quit.

How Do You Define Success?

Before you think I'm trying to water down the idea of success to allow you to feel better (less bad) about failing—I'm not. But I do want to expand the normal definition of success a bit.

The American Heritage Dictionary defines *success* as "the achievement of something desired, planned, or attempted." Fair enough. That is certainly the most common way to look at success in our modern world. For instance, Henry Ward Beecher said, "It is not the going out of port, but the coming in, that determines the success of a voyage." From a number of perspectives, that's true—especially where it concerns profit or loss in business. If the ship sinks the business may fail.

But when I look closer at the dictionary I notice a definition I rather like more—one that is, unfortunately, labeled "obsolete:" "a result or an outcome." As I understand the difference between the contemporary definition and the "obsolete" one, the latter allows the possibility for "results" and "outcomes" not originally intended. And it's in that gray area the inventors and scientists I described earlier found success. They all discovered something for which they weren't looking.

The contemporary definition of success seems to me to be consistent with the technological, digital, binary-based world we live in where things are either on or off. You either fail or succeed. In real life, however, things are not just on or off. There are many outcomes and results along the path to a goal, or the path of life, that can be counted as entirely beneficial, productive, satisfying, and life altering.

What I like best about the "outcomes and results" way of looking at success is that it allows for two very important factors: the passage of time and the intervention of God. I have already said several times and in several ways that the journey of life is the true destination; that passage of time in which we come to know the God who created us and with whom we will spend eternity. Time allows God the opportunity to teach us about ourselves, to take us through experiences which help show us who we are and why we need Him.

I like what B. C. Forbes, the 1917 founder of *Forbes* magazine and publishing business, said about time and success: "For my part, I rather distrust men or concerns that rise up with the speed of rockets. Sudden rises are sometimes followed by equally sudden falls. I have most faith in the individual or enterprise that advances step by step. A mushroom can spring up in a day; an oak takes fifty years or more to reach maturity. Mushrooms don't last; oaks do. The real cause for an enormous number of business failures is premature over-expansion, attempting to gallop before learning to creep. Sudden successes often invite sudden reverses." (Goodman, Ted, ed. *The Forbes Book of Business Quotations. 14,173 Thoughts on the Business of Life*. New York: Black Dog & Levanthal Publishers, Inc., 1997, p. 801.)

Time allows for the development of character and opportunity as well, as seen in another recollection from the same legendary publisher: "The very first task given Harvey D. Gibson on entering the Boston office of the American Express Co., when he left college, was to shoulder a couple of knapsacks—after he finished sweeping the floor—and deliver bundles of canceled checks to local banks. The first bundle he delivered was from the Liberty National Bank of New York. Fifteen years later he became president of this same bank.

"Had he scorned to sweep the floor, as being beneath the dignity of a college-bred youth, is it likely that he would be where he is today?" B. C. Forbes's answer was probably, "Not very."

One of my first jobs was in the maintenance department of my father's church. In other words, I was a janitor: I cleaned and polished toilets and mirrors and bathroom floors. While it was a humbling job, I learned that the appearance of the bathrooms was as important as any other aspect of the ministry. Now, as the senior pastor of that same church, I have a much deeper appreciation for those who do the "invisible" jobs behind the scenes. We are not preparing sermons or cleaning toilets or cutting grass or sending out mailings. We're building the kingdom of God.

More than time, character, talent, or any other ingredient, I believe God is the greatest and most underutilized ingredient for success (results and outcomes) in our world. I love the description of young David's success as found in 1 Samuel 18:14: "In everything he did he had great success, because the LORD was with him." I'm going to stretch the meaning of that statement to make a point: It didn't matter what

David chose to do. With God as His guide/companion/friend, David was successful.

Saul, who was descending from the throne of Israel as David was ascending to it, was entirely frustrated with David's success. In fact, "When Saul saw how successful [David] was, he was afraid of him" (v. 15). In the big picture, God made the difference in Saul's decline and David's rise. Saul disobeyed God and God abandoned him (see 1 Sam. 15:28) and turned to David. Without God, Saul's life was marked by negative results and outcomes: jealousy, fear, and mental and emotional instability. With God, David's life was marked by the opposite. (Almost) all of his results and outcomes were positive.

Can you imagine any greater potential for success in life than being in a life-partnership with the very God who formed you in your mother's womb—who knows you better than you know yourself—who wrote all your days in His book before you began to live them (see Ps. 139:13–16)? Honestly, I can't.

That's why I like to define success in terms that include God, time, flexibility, satisfaction, surprises, and growth—all in varying degrees as we move through life. Thinking of success that way—especially knowing how much God is "for" my having an abundant life (see John 10:10)—allows me to take more seriously the ideas, desires, and dreams I have.

Good Ideas vs. God's Ideas

I often wonder why people who are in a loving, satisfying relationship with God through Jesus Christ don't give God more credit for the good ideas they have. I mean that in a way that's probably different from what you're thinking.

I don't mean "credit" in the sense that it's plagiarism if we don't give God credit; as if He's a self-centered deity who can't stand for someone to take credit for what He did. Instead, I mean credit this way: Often when we have a great idea for our lives, something we feel really passionate about, a dream we can't seem to shake, we say, "Oh, that's just another one of my pie-in-the-sky ideas. I could never do that; that could never happen." And we go on living in the dream of that idea rather than in its reality.

Instead, we should say this: "God, because I know You love me to be excited about our life together, I'm going to believe this idea is from You. Or, at least until You show me it's not. Thank You for this idea, Father! Please nurture it in my heart and keep it alive if this is something You want me to do."

See the difference? I just don't think many people live in the reality of life as a God-with-us experience. I challenge you to begin giving God credit for your ideas and dreams and desires—the ones that would maximize your potential and bring glory to Him at the same time. Stop leaving God out of the process! If your ideas are really His ideas in you, is it really beyond your faith to believe He will help you achieve something He put in your heart to do?

Just one step of faith on your part might lead to something more satisfying than you have ever imagined (see Eph. 3:20).

At the same time I was ordained into the ministry at the Crystal Cathedral, I was installed in my first ministry position: minister of evangelism. I was given a spacious office on the eleventh floor of the Tower of Hope on the church's campus. For all intents and purposes, it seemed like an ideal setting in which to begin my ministry. But within a few months I heard God's call to leave.

There were no problems with my assignment at the church. I just believed God wanted me to start a new church. So I resigned and spent the next twenty years building the Rancho Capistrano Community Church in San Juan Capistrano, California. Today the Ranch, as it is commonly called, is home to the church, a school, and a retreat center. It sits on a hundred-acre estate nestled into the hills of a beautiful coastal community and touches the lives of thousands of people.

In that case, God's idea turned out to be a very good idea.

Success in Motion

No one will argue that John Grisham is a successful novelist. In fact, he's the most commercially successful novelist of the last two decades with more than one hundred million books in print in thirty-one languages and seven of his complicated legal dramas being made into Hollywood movies. But Grisham's success didn't happen overnight.

His first novel, *A Time to Kill*, was rejected by twenty-eight agents and publishers. When a publisher finally accepted it, the initial press run was only five thousand copies with little marketing investment. So Grisham bought one thousand copies from the publisher and traveled from bookstore to bookstore with a trunk full of books trying to get the owners interested. It was only after his second novel hit the best-seller list that momentum began to swing his way. Now, initial press runs of a new Grisham book run in the millions.

It was not momentum that launched John Grisham's career as a novelist; it was motion. If he hadn't gotten in his car and visited those bookstores to help generate a buzz about his first book, his success might have been a different story.

God gives us ideas but it is up to us to take the steps to see those dreams become realities. It is far easier for God to direct us toward the fulfillment of our dreams when we are moving. Turning the rudder on a ship doesn't change the ship's direction until energy is applied. Turning your eyes to look at your dream is one thing; turning your feet to pursue it is another.

I challenge you to put yourself in motion for the sake of your dreams. Do something; do anything! Express your faith by moving so God can come alongside and provide course corrections as you go.

Give yourself the freedom to think of the world as your playground.

Every Day Is Recess

At a typical grammar school, when the kids burst out of the school doors and head for the playground at recess, what do they do? *They do whatever they want within the bounds of the playground and the school rules.* Without anyone telling them what to do, some run for the swings, some for the jungle gym, some for the slide, and some for the merry-go-round. Others jump rope, play jacks on the sidewalk, or throw a Frisbee. Still others race for the ball fields to play softball or kickball.

Why do they make these choices? Because it's what brings them joy at recess and they know they're free to choose how to spend their precious thirty minutes of freedom. Okay, peer pressure and friendships may steer some of the kids in one direction or the other, but for purposes of our discussion let's assume they are fulfilling their longings by the activity they choose at recess.

I'm not sure why we don't think of life this way, but I believe we should. Those children have a designated area in which to play and general guidelines of courtesy and safety to follow. Within those two limitations they can do whatever they want. Our playground is planet Earth and our guidelines are God's moral stipulations that are for our own good. Within those boundaries, we are free to do whatever we want!

That doesn't negate the idea of God's purpose or calling for our lives. Just as a teacher might come alongside and influence a student to adjust his or her activity, I believe God is perfectly capable of working within our choices to cause us to fulfill the purpose He knows will suit us best.

Our challenge is to look at life as our playground and every day as recess; to take off the blinders and dream bigger and farther than we've ever dreamed before. And give God credit for being creative enough to work within our "fun" to accomplish His purposes.

History Doesn't Repeat Itself

You have heard many times, "Those who don't learn from history are doomed to repeat it." Let me add a twist to that thought by saying that history doesn't repeat itself—we do. But let me also note that we are not obligated to repeat anything.

If you wasted the last ten years of your life, you are not destined to waste the next ten. If you come from a family of ne'er-do-wells, you are not destined to be a ne'er-do-well. If there is sexual, substance, or physical abuse in your past—as a victim or participant—none of those traits has to be in your future. People can and do change. And you can be one of those people.

Dr. Robert O. Young is a microbiologist who has shaken up traditional theories of disease and health with his pleomorphic views of microforms in the human body. *Pleo* means "many" and *morph* means "form." Therefore, *pleomorphic* means "many-formed"—the idea that red blood cells in the body, as well as other microforms, can mutate (change) into unhealthy forms—bacteria, yeast, fungus—in an unhealthy inner-body environment. They can morph (change) from good to bad and back again simply by changing the body's inner terrain (making it unhealthy or healthy).

I want to borrow his term and suggest that you and I live pleomorphic lives, meaning we are able to change continually. We are not static, stuck in the form we inherited from our parents' histories, genes, or experiences. Our success (results and outcomes) can change as we alter the inner, spiritual terrain of our lives and begin to think God's thoughts after him.

God once told the nation of Israel He would make up for them the years the locusts had eaten (see Joel 2:25). Where the land had been laid waste, God would refresh and restore. Where their barns had been empty, God would refill. Where their hearts had been broken, God would apply His balm. Israel was not stuck in their past—the future was a brand-new day.

Believe that you are a pleomorphic person, able to change into the person you want to be, by the grace of God and with His help.

Writing Your Future History

I challenge you to begin thinking differently about success in your life. Think about how you define it. Give God credit for the dreams about which you are passionate but assume can't happen. Start moving so God can guide you. Give yourself permission from God to do what you want to do within the best-for-you boundaries He has clearly established. And break free from the past. You are not bound to repeat anything you don't want to.

Above all, believe that God wants you to experience results and outcomes that satisfy you to depths you've never imagined. He only asks that you make Him your partner in the process.

What do we need to take with us on our journey (Christ, confidence, courage, etc.)?

Be Prepared

> Therefore, since we are surrounded by such a great cloud of witnesses, let us throw off everything that hinders and the sin that so easily entangles, and let us run with perseverance the race marked out for us. Let us fix our eyes on Jesus, the author and perfecter of our faith.
>
> —Hebrews 12:1–2

Shannon Smith was due to report for freshmen orientation at her college in two weeks. She and her parents used their guest bedroom as a staging area for collecting everything she would need for her first year at college.

The "stuff" Shannon put together to take to school filled the top of the queen-sized bed and was overflowing onto the floor. Her checklist was taped to the door, and for the last several days she had been methodically checking things off as she and her mother collected the items.

Shannon's dad, Steve, stopped at the door on Saturday afternoon as she was organizing things and let out a low whistle: "Maybe it would have been easier just to put the things you're not planning to take in here. That way, on the day we leave, we could just load up everything that's not in this room. What do you think?"

"Very funny, Dad. I'm trying to be careful—I know I only have half the dorm room."

That night, Shannon and her parents were at the kitchen table finishing supper. "You know, sweetie," her dad said, looking at Shannon, "I've been thinking about the checklist on the door of the bedroom. I've been mulling over the idea of a second checklist I think you ought to create before you leave for college."

"What kind of list?" Shannon asked. "I thought I had everything on my list upstairs."

"Well, here's what I'm thinking," her dad said as he leaned forward, setting his coffee cup on the table. "The things you have on your list upstairs are what you'll need to live your physical life, your outer life—and you've done a good job getting everything together. But I'm thinking about what you'll need to live your inner life. You know, things like beliefs and values and priorities. I think it might be a good exercise to make a list; to treat those things with the same importance as the things for your physical life."

"I'm not sure what you'd want me to put on a list like that," Shannon said.

"Well, why don't you mull it over for a few days and we'll talk about it next weekend? Think of it this way: What beliefs and commitments and priorities—the things that make Shannon who she is—do you think you should take to college with you? Things without which you might find yourself in trouble; things as important as your toothbrush and laundry detergent are to your physical life. You'll think of some things. Why don't you shoot for, say, five things you need to have in your heart as you leave for college?"

Nobody mentioned the list during the following week, but the next Saturday morning Shannon came into the kitchen with a piece of paper in her hand. "I've got the list you asked me to write," she said. "Do you want to see it?"

"Why don't you read it to us?" her mom said. "Let's sit down."

Once they were at the table, Shannon began: "I'm not sure this is the kind of stuff you were talking about," she said, "but here goes—I've got five things.

"First, I need to take my relationship with God. And since I'm leaving home and our church I need to find a church home at school, or a campus Bible study, or something, to keep my spiritual life strong.

"Next, I put down relationships with others. By that I mean making choices of friends, especially guys, that will reinforce my beliefs and not tear them down.

"The next thing is to live in a way that honors my family. You all are

sacrificing to send me to college and I don't want to take that for granted. I know I'm still accountable to you for my activities until I'm out on my own someday, and even though you won't be looking over my shoulder at school I want to honor what I know you expect from me.

"Fourth is to have my own personal honor code about school—to be honest about how I approach my studies and to do the best I can in my classes.

"Finally, I put down faith and courage. I imagine I may get lonely or scared at times, or even have to say no to temptations—and I want to not be afraid; to not call you every time something's wrong but to learn to trust God to help me when I need strength.

"What do you think?" she said, looking at her mom and dad, who were sitting silently.

"Well, I think I wish I had been as prepared for college when I left home as I think you are," her mom said, breaking the silence. "That's an amazing list, Shannon."

"I agree," her dad said. "I felt in my heart you were ready for this journey. But after hearing your list, I know you are."

THOSE OF US WHO TRAVEL consistently in connection with our vocation probably have our preparation routine pretty well established. We can throw a bag together in an hour's time if needed: tickets/itinerary, clothes, toiletries, laptop, cell phone/PDA, books/papers, contacts book, and personal items (headphones, energy bars, reading/work material, and the like). International trips require a bit more planning: passport, voltage converters for electronic gadgets, medicines, vitamins, multi-zone clock. All in all, preparation for a personal trip is routine.

The same cannot be said, however, for other kinds of trips. Take what may be, outside of climbing Mount Everest, the most grueling feat of human endurance on the planet, the Iditarod Trail Sled Dog Race, usually called "the Iditarod" for short. Because I love to read about people doing the impossible, I've read about this race through the years just to remind myself that the impossible is doable. Besides endurance, perseverance, withstanding pain, and other lessons, I'm blown away by the amount of preparation each participant has to make. In the words of one race participant I read about, "Preparation for next year's race begins on the day this year's race ends." This is not a case of "throwing a bag together in an hour" and grabbing a cab to the airport.

The race starts on the first Saturday of March each year and consists of individuals driving ("mushing") their dogs and sleds approximately 1,150 miles from Anchorage to Nome, Alaska. That would be challenging enough under ideal conditions, but the racers frequently encounter "whiteout" conditions—snow and gale-force winds causing the wind chill factor to plummet to –100 degrees F!

The preparations for such a test go on all year long. In other words, for "Iditarodders," *life is an ongoing process of preparation.* The nine to fifteen days of the actual race are merely a way to evaluate how well they prepared over the previous eleven and a half months. For instance, a racers' thirty or more dogs, from which the final team will be selected, require daily attention: food, exercise, play, training, and relationship-building between the driver and the dogs—maybe the most critical aspect of all.

Generally speaking, the first half of the year is focused on training the dogs, with the second half devoted to preparatory races and preparing supplies and equipment for the Iditarod. For instance, every racer has to prepare about two thousand pounds of food for the dogs (each dog burns up to ten thousand calories a day). The food is bagged, frozen, and shipped to twenty checkpoints along the race trail where each team picks it up "on the go"—the ultimate version of fast food.

And strategy is key. There are some required periods of rest, but for the most part racers are free to race and rest as they see fit. Most follow a "six-on, six-off" plan (six hours of racing followed by six hours of rest) because the dogs' efficiency falls off after six or seven hours of hard pulling. Races have been won and lost in the past on the basis of strategy—when to run and when to rest.

I could go on and on about the superhuman feat of preparing for and participating in the Iditarod. While the details are fascinating, the principle that most impresses me is that life for Iditarod racers is in a constant, year-round state of preparation. This is true for many endurance athletes, of course, and is the reason why the apostle Paul used athletic training metaphors in picturing what it takes to run the spiritual race successfully:

> Do you not know that in a race all the runners run, but only one gets the prize? Run in such a way as to get the prize. Everyone who competes in the games goes into strict training. They do it to get a crown that will not last; but we do it to get a crown that will last forever. Therefore I do not run like a man running aimlessly; I do not fight like a man beating the air. No, I beat my body and make it my slave so that after I have preached to others, I myself will not be disqualified for the prize. (1 Corinthians 9:24–27)

I love his expressions "like a man running aimlessly . . . like a man beating the air." That would be the equivalent of someone showing up for the Iditarod on the first Friday in March wearing shades and a Polartec vest with a dozen neighborhood dogs (poodles, Labs, mutts, pugs) tied to a Red Flyer wagon and a bag of Wendy's burgers saying, "Where do I register?" That would be the epitome of what's called "unclear on the concept."

Do we attempt to live life that way at times—failing to make adequate preparations—and then wondering why we don't achieve the success for which we hoped? Based on conversations with multitudes of people through the years, I think the chances of that happening are good.

There was a small segment of my life during which I spent years in the preparation phase: marlin fishing. I caught my first marlin off the coast of Mexico but could not repeat my good fortune when I began looking for them off the coast of Southern California. They were there—I just couldn't catch them. I went out at least fifteen times, all day, and came back with no marlin each time. But every time I went I was learning about the ocean and what was in it—learning to "read" the sea. I would fish deep and shallow using this line and lure or that. No results, but learning (preparing) all the time. I knew eventually I would catch this phantom of the ocean.

And I did. With the help of others more experienced, in time I became proficient and began to catch marlin. I was part of a team that even caught five in one day in southern California. But it took years to see that happen. Preparation and education always bring results if we have the patience to wait.

We don't do badly at preparing for the physical, external side of life. We get a measure of education and then move into a vocation. We buy insurance, try to save a little for the future, and keep things on an even keel as our journey through life progresses. In fact, as challenging as the external aspects of life can be at times, I actually think they're relatively easy—because they have to do with "things."

It's making internal, spiritual preparations for life we tend to avoid. Indeed, I find many people will fill up their lives with "things" just to keep from pausing long enough to think about their inner lives. That's easy to do, especially in the first half of life when we feel invincible—like we can conquer the world. But when we enter the second half of life, certainly in our sixties and seventies, we've usually learned that all our physical preparations haven't provided the answers to life's hardest questions: What has been the purpose of my life? Who will miss me when I'm gone? How do I prepare for the end of life—and how will it end? What kind of legacy will I leave behind? And, perhaps most important, what will happen to me when I die? We start thinking more about significance and less about success.

If I could sum up my role as a pastor, it might best be stated in terms of helping people make the necessary preparations for the living (and ending) of temporal and eternal life. As I've stated already in this book, life takes a circuitous route; it's filled with twists and turns no one can predict—except for the final page we call death. To the best of my knowledge, 100 percent of us arrive at that final appointment—sooner or later. The only way I know to complete such a journey successfully is to make adequate preparation. Like the Iditarod racers, preparation becomes a full-time job, a lifelong process.

Spiritual preparation of life is not nearly as complex as many imagine. I've learned that most of what we need to know can be thought of as three gifts we ought to give ourselves. Like a three-legged stool, they're all important—take one away and things fall over in a hurry. Keep all three in place and you're ready to face anything life offers.

The Gift of Perspective

Charles Lindbergh's place in American and aviation history was sealed on May 20–21, 1927, as the first person to fly solo and nonstop from New York to Paris. The single-engine plane in which he made the thirty-three-hour flight, *The Spirit of St. Louis*, now hangs overhead in the National Air and Space Museum, part of the Smithsonian Institution.

In 1997, Lindbergh's daughter, Reeve, was invited to deliver the annual Lindbergh Address at the museum in honor of the seventieth anniversary of her father's famous flight. In order for her to have the opportunity to inspect her father's plane, the organizers invited her to come ahead of the gathering crowd.

When she arrived, Reeve Lindbergh and her young son, Ben, were lifted some twenty feet off the ground in the bucket of a cherry-picker so they could literally reach out and touch the plane. Being at eye level with her father's craft was an emotional experience for Reeve. She had never touched the plane before. She gently ran her hand along the fuselage, touching the door handle she knew her father touched so many times before.

With tears in her eyes she whispered to her son, "Oh, Ben, isn't this amazing?"

"Yeeeaaaaaah," Ben replied with a sense of awe. "I've never been in a cherry-picker before!"

From the mouths of children, right? The first time I read that story I immediately thought of "my thoughts are not your thoughts" (Isa. 55:8). Young Ben and his mom obviously had two different perspectives on the same event.

There are two ways of looking at our lives as well: our way and God's way. And the words God spoke through Isaiah the prophet are worthy of our consideration. There's an important progression from verse 8 to verse 9 in Isaiah 55. Verse 8 says God's thoughts and our thoughts are different. But note what verse 9 says: "As the heavens are higher than the earth, so are my ways higher than your ways and my thoughts than your thoughts."

When I was thirteen my father and I built a small cabin in the mountains near Moonridge, California. We spent many getaway days and nights· there. One summer when I was sixteen I was looking out the window of the cabin at the surrounding mountain peaks and decided I would climb to the top of the highest one. Putting on my tennis shoes I began the ascent.

After a harder-than-expected climb, I reached the summit only to discover it wasn't the summit at all. It was merely a peak hiding the real summit from my vantage point in the cabin. So I went back down to the valley floor and started up a different peak, expecting it to be the tallest peak. Same thing—it was another smaller peak behind which loomed the largest one, the true summit.

Life is a lot like that. We often cannot see the next peak God has for us until we are willing to climb the one closest to us. My father calls it the "peak to peek" way of looking at life. It's another way of recognizing that not only are God's thoughts different from ours, they are higher as well.

To use human terms, we look at life as if we're standing on a hilltop or mountaintop—not a bad view, but nowhere near as good as God's. He looks at life from a higher plane, heaven to be exact. While we can see a bit of where we've been and a bit of where we're going, there's always the horizon we can't see over. But there are no horizons from where God sits. He sees our entire life as one event—past, present, and future.

But with the coming of Jesus to this world, the Father still had the big picture but the Son was now living a human life on earth, like us. He was tempted, got hungry and tired, had to relieve Himself, had to deal with self-centered and sinful people, and had to do things—especially one BIG thing—He might have preferred not to do. In essence, "Although [Jesus] was a son, he learned obedience from what he suffered" (Heb. 5:8).

That doesn't mean "he learned the hard way," like we do. It means that, through the things He suffered, He learned obedience to God. He learned to prioritize and to choose. He learned that self's goals aren't as good as God's goals. He learned what was really important in life. And He learned that great good comes from pain and hardship.

Even though Jesus has returned to the Father in heaven, there is a mysterious mix of perspectives there now. Because of Jesus' time on earth, the Bible says this: "For we do not have a high priest who is unable to sympathize with our weaknesses, but we have one who has been tempted in every way, just as we are—yet was without sin. Let us then approach the throne of grace with confidence, so that we may receive mercy and find grace to help us in our time of need" (Heb. 4:15–16). In addition, "Because he himself suffered when he was tempted, he is able to help those who are being tempted" (Heb. 2:18)—and that would be us.

So now when Jesus talks to the Father on our behalf (see 1 John 2:1), He speaks about life on earth with firsthand knowledge. And when we call out to God in prayer for help, the Spirit of God prays through us as if it were Jesus calling out to the Father from here on earth (see Rom. 8:26–27).

So, for two reasons, I encourage you to give yourself the gift of God's perspective on your life. Not only does He have the better view, He has lived the earthly life you're trying to live—and lived to tell about it.

The Gift of Life

But to get God's perspective on your life you have to have a working relationship with Him. And for that you need to give yourself the gift of life—spiritual life. By that I mean you have to have a relationship with God that "begins" at a point in time.

Like many things, we have succeeded in making what it means to know God more complicated than it is. I think Jesus' metaphor of new birth has never been improved upon because it draws the perfect parallel between physical and spiritual birth. Jesus said, "No one can see the kingdom of God unless he is born again" (John 3:3). "Flesh gives birth to flesh," He said, "But the Spirit gives birth to spirit" (v. 6). Just as we were born physically, so we have to be born again spiritually. No one "evolves" into a relationship with God. It requires a choice and a commitment based on God's terms. And those terms require making a decision to take Jesus at His word about who He is (Savior) and why He came to earth (to save those who are lost).

Too often, the "born again" language about not seeing the kingdom of God gets relegated to heaven only. But I don't think that's all it means. The kingdom of God is growing and expanding on earth as we speak. Like a mustard seed, it started small but is growing larger all the time (see Matt. 13:31). The kingdom of God is His authority and His rule. Every time someone on earth yields to God's authority and accepts His rule of their life, the kingdom grows. So, "seeing the kingdom of God," in born-again terms, has as much to do with seeing God's perspective on life on earth as much as in heaven.

If someone asked you, "What is the most important story Jesus Christ ever told?" what would you say? He told lots of intriguing parables, but He said there was one that was the key to all the rest. That award goes to the parable in Matthew 13:1–23, what we call the parable of the sower/soils/seeds—the parable about the sower who sows seeds that fell on four different kinds of soils: the hard-packed path, rocky soil, soil where thorns grew, and good, rich soil.

In the version of this parable in Mark's Gospel, he records Jesus as reproving the disciples about their failure to understand this parable: "Then Jesus said to them, 'Don't you understand this parable? How then will you understand any parable?'" (Mark 4:13). In my mind, that last question makes the parable of the soils the most important story Jesus told.

Why is this parable the key to all the rest of the parables? Because it's about life in God's kingdom—the same kingdom Jesus said we can't see unless we're born again.

Matthew grouped Jesus' seven parables about the kingdom together in Matthew 13:1–52. And they all begin with this phrase: "The kingdom of heaven is like . . ." All except the first one, that is—the one about the soils; the one Jesus said was the key to the others. The parable of the four soils doesn't begin with "The kingdom of heaven is like" because it's not about defining the kingdom—it's about understanding the kingdom; about living in the kingdom; about receiving truth about the kingdom. It's not just about the kingdom in heaven, it's about the kingdom on earth; the same kingdom Jesus prayed would come to earth in the prayer He taught the disciples: "Your kingdom come, your will be done on earth as it is in heaven" (Matt. 6:10).

Are you with me on this? God's kingdom is His rule; His perspective. If you want to see God's kingdom, His perspective, you have to be born again. Jesus said it's non-negotiable: "You must be born again" (John 3:7).

In the parable of the soils, Jesus said the seed sown by the farmer represents "the message about the kingdom" (Matt. 13:19). In other words, when you hear God's truth, as conveyed to us in the Bible, you are hearing a "message about the kingdom"—a message about God's perspective on this life. But four different things can happen to that message: God's enemy, the devil, can snatch it away if your heart is too hard to accept it. You can believe it today but throw it away tomorrow because God doesn't rescue you immediately when trouble hits. Or you can believe it today but walk away from it tomorrow because you're lured away by the world's enticements.

Or, you can receive and believe that seed and allow it to spring up in your heart and bear abundant fruit, leading you to have ears that hear and eyes that see God's perspective on your life (see Matt. 13:13).

That, of course, is the kind of soil (heart) Jesus recommends. I can't imagine walking on a journey through this life without the benefit of having new life; without the benefit of His perspective on my past, present, and future. If you don't have a relationship with God, or even if you're not sure whether you do or not, I encourage you to begin such a relationship today by receiving the gift of life He offers. Jesus said, "I am the way and the truth and the *life*. No one comes to the Father except through me" (John 14:6; emphasis added). When you receive Christ as your Lord and Savior, you get the gift of new life. It's as if you've been "born again"—and you have!

I pray you'll prepare for the rest of your life by allowing yourself to receive the gift of eternal life.

When I was eight years old my father took me to hear Billy Graham in the Los Angeles Coliseum. The Crystal Cathedral was called Garden Grove Community Church at that time—a congregation of a few hundred members. My father wasn't on television then and had written no best-sellers. We sat in the bleachers along with everyone else. Even though I was raised in the church, knew all the Bible stories, and knew

I wanted to be a preacher when I grew up, when Billy Graham gave the invitation for people to go forward and dedicate their lives to Christ, I knew he was talking to me.

I asked my dad if I could go forward and, of course, he said I could. I remember it like it was yesterday. A counselor talked and prayed with me and I gave my life to Christ. I was born again at the Los Angeles Coliseum.

The Gift of Love

Just as Jesus had a most important story, Paul had a most important value. It's this value I hope you'll make the third gift you give yourself.

Many people are familiar with Paul's famous words in 1 Corinthians 13:13: "And now these three remain: faith, hope and love. But the greatest of these is love." Rather than taking those words as a religious platitude, I think we should take them literally: love is the most important value in the universe. When God sent His own Son to earth to give the gift of life to lost souls, He didn't do it on the basis of faith or hope: "God *so loved* the world that he *gave* . . ." (John 3:16).

Love isn't a feeling; it is a choice revealed in an action. God *so loved* that He *gave*. When we become people of love it will become apparent because of our actions. To be prepared for the rest of your life, there are three dimensions in which love needs to be expressed:

Love for God. This is at the heart of the previous point. Jesus said the greatest law known to man is to "love the Lord your God with all your heart and with all your soul and with all your mind" (Matt. 22:37). That's the essence of being a Christian. Whatever we love changes in our estimation. If God has not occupied a significant place in your life, it may be because you have not loved Him. Give your affections to Him, and your perception of Him, and His importance in your life, will change.

Love for Self. Too many people can't love themselves because they don't love the God who created them. When you love God your estimation of the value of what He has created will change—and that includes you. You can't love God and hate yourself, either for who you are or what you have done (the two main reasons people can't accept and love themselves). God created you and He forgives you. Therefore, if you love Him you will love His creation and His act of forgiveness for everything you have ever done.

Love for Others. Too many people can't love others because they don't love themselves (because they don't love God). But when you release yourself from your self-imposed limitations (because you know God places no limitations on you) you are free to love others. You have a heart and hands that are filled with actions that bless and benefit others. People stop becoming obstacles to what you are trying to accomplish and start becoming accomplices in the great, mysterious, and worshipful drama God is working out in your life. And you can't wait to see the role "this person" is going to play.

Prepare for life! Don't try to wing it—you've already discovered the results of such a worldview. Give yourself the gift of God's perspective, the gift of God's life, and the gift of God's love. I have yet to encounter anything in my own life for which these three gifts did not prove to be the exact preparation I needed. And I believe your experience will be the same.

*What obstacles must
we be prepared to overcome
(doubt, criticism, fear, etc.)?*

Potholes and Pitfalls

If the LORD delights in a man's way, he makes his steps firm; though he stumble, he will not fall, for the LORD upholds him with his hand.

—Psalm 37:23–24

Jeremy Anderson was eighteen, a senior in high school, on 9-11-2001. Since he was a nationally ranked long-distance runner on his high school track team, his coach assured him there would be track scholarship offers coming from more than one major university. But when 9-11 happened Jeremy began to question what was most important: going to college and running track or doing his part to defend his country.

He came from a patriotic family—his dad was a career army officer, seeing action in the first Gulf War. Now retired and in a second career, he was still a strong influence on Jeremy. If the nation needed their son, John Anderson and his wife were not opposed to him serving.

The question was, how? Rather than react impulsively and enlist in the army when he graduated from high school in May 2002 John counseled Jeremy to wait and see what developed. Would America go only to Afghanistan in search of Osama bin Laden, or would the talk of invading Iraq gain momentum? American and British forces began aerial attacks on Afghanistan less than a month after 9-11. No one knew whether other actions would occur and a surge in troop strength would be needed.

So Jeremy signed a track scholarship with his state university and enrolled as a freshman in September 2002. And, as expected, he immediately made the varsity squad in the long-distance categories. His love for track and for his long-term goal of coaching track and field at the university level just grew stronger.

But he lived that first semester of school with an eye and ear tuned to the talks in Washington about "the war on terror." It became clear that America was going to invade Iraq—an invasion commencing in March 2003—the spring of Jeremy's freshman year. He decided it was time to enlist. He would finish his freshman year, sign up for a two-year army stint, then return to school.

Less than a year later, Jeremy found himself on the outskirts of Baghdad, Iraq. The invasion toppled Saddam Hussein's dictatorship and the messy job of "winning the peace" was the order of the day. And it wasn't going well. Terrorist insurgents were flooding into the area to take advantage of the political and military instability. And it was one of their strikes that changed Jeremy's life.

While on patrol with his unit, an RPG (rocket-propelled grenade) ripped through the Humvee in which he was riding and severed Jeremy from his future—or so he thought. It was only the excellent army emergency field hospital that saved his life—though they couldn't save his legs. At age twenty, Jeremy Anderson—track star and future track coach—found himself without his legs from just below the knee down.

Four years later, Jeremy Anderson was being honored by his university as the athlete of the year. Standing on stage in a suit, the audience couldn't see his high-tech titanium lower "legs" and "feet." Only a slightly halting gait as he walked to the podium gave a hint he was any different at all. His remarks were what set him apart from the crowd.

"I'm so grateful for the opportunity I've had to continue my involvement with track and field," he said. "When I was injured in Iraq, all I could think about for months was that my life, and what I loved most, was over. I had never had an obstacle like this put in front of me before, and it definitely changed things. But once I got my shiny new legs and feet, and started getting used to them, things began to look different.

"I might not run and win races anymore, but thanks to our coaches, and the university, I've discovered that I can still make a contribution to the track program. Being able to stay involved in developing training programs, *scouting high school runners, and working with our incoming recruits has been an awesome way to stay involved in the sport I love.*

"More than anything, I discovered that the greatest obstacle to my having a career in track and field was not being without legs and feet. The greatest obstacle would be not to have the courage to pursue my dream. Without heart, a perfectly healthy runner can become a loser. But even without legs, a runner with heart can be a winner. And with God's help, that's what I hope to be."

HARLAN WAS BORN on September 9, 1890, into a hardscrabble existence. Henryville, Indiana, was as plain a place as a plain young boy could be born—and that's what Harlan was. His father labored in the Kentucky coal mines to support a family of seven, but died when Harlan was just six years old. His mother took a job in a garment factory which left the task of caring for his siblings—including doing much of the cooking—to Harlan, the oldest of the five.

When his mother remarried, Harlan and his stepfather didn't see eye-to-eye, so he hit the road—at the ripe old age of twelve. For the next twenty-five years his life was a work in progress; he failed at more jobs during that period than most people will ever try. With little guidance and less education, he was making life up as he went along. He worked as a farm hand, a streetcar conductor, a private in the U.S. Army in Cuba (he lied about his age to join), a blacksmith's apprentice, a rail-yard fireman for Southern Railway, a ferryboat captain, an insurance sales-man, a tire salesman, and a service station manager for Standard Oil. He also studied law by correspondence. And in the midst of his vocational success, he married at eighteen and had a child.

But then he found something he was good at. In 1930, in the middle of the Great Depression, in a service station he managed in Kentucky, he started preparing and serving meals. He pumped gas, cooked food, ran the cash register—the epitome of the proverbial "chief cook and bottle washer." But it worked. Maybe it was his early training at the stove as a child, cooking for his siblings. Whatever it was, people liked his food—especially his fried chicken.

They liked it so much the word spread and he actually began to make money. He expanded Sanders Court and Café to include a motel and a restaurant seating 142 people. In 1936 he was awarded the honorary rank of "Kentucky Colonel" by the governor of the state in recognition of his contribution to the state's cuisine.

The entire place burned down in 1939, but Colonel Sanders rebuilt it and pressed forward. That year was momentous for more than the fire. When Colonel Sanders attended a demonstration of a new kitchen device called a pressure cooker, he wondered if he could use it to speed up the process of preparing chicken. When he put his chicken, coated with his secret recipe of eleven herbs and spices, in the pressure cooker, it was a "Eureka!" moment. In 1940 his "original recipe" chicken was born.

Colonel Sanders began traveling the country demonstrating his pressure-cooked, secret-spiced chicken to restaurant owners. For the princely sum of five cents for every chicken they cooked, he would teach them his pressure-cooker technique and furnish them with his secret spice recipe. And the franchise idea was born. In 1952 the first franchise went to a restaurant owner in Utah, a clever man who came up with the name "Kentucky Fried Chicken" and the Colonel's trademark white suit.

Just as it looked like things couldn't get anything but better, in 1955 Interstate 75 was built through eastern Kentucky, bypassing the small town of Corbin. The colonel's motel and restaurant traffic disappeared within months of the freeway's opening, and he was forced to sell everything. After settling his bills, Colonel Harlan Sanders was penniless at age sixty-five.

When his first Social Security check arrived in the mail—$105—he was so insulted that he decided he wouldn't quit. With his (second) wife mixing and bagging spices at home, he hit the road again with his pressure cooker. Within five years there were four hundred restaurants selling Kentucky Fried Chicken, and six hundred by 1964.

That year, the Colonel turned seventy-five years old. And when a group of Kentucky investors offered him $2 million for the franchise, he took the deal, remaining as the white-suited, white-goateed spokesman known around the world today.

The company has changed hands several times since 1964, but today more than a billion KFC meals are served annually in over eighty countries around the world. The man who spent the better part of his life overcoming obstacles to success finally found, at age sixty-five, his calling and passion in life.

There are several reasons the story of Harlan Sanders is worth telling. But being a great spiritual story is not one of them. It is not a story about conversion or new birth late in life. I don't know what Harlan Sanders's spiritual perspective on life was. But for this book, it doesn't matter. There are other reasons why his story is valuable.

First, it is a story that reminds us life is hard. I won't insult your intelligence or your experience by pretending to tell you something you don't already know. But I will remind you, and myself, that life is difficult. Sometimes we forget what happened in the Garden of Eden millennia ago. God cursed the earth because of Adam and Eve's sin. It would only be through "painful toil" and "the sweat of [our] brow" that we would reap anything from it (Gen. 3:17–19). I know—we have cars and microwaves and dry cleaning and food to eat that someone else sweats over in the field. But is there anyone among us who would say, in spite of those advancements, that life is not hard? You will not hear that from me. The grace of God has not removed the "hardness" from life for the Christian, even though it gives us reason to hope in the midst of it. Hope and grace have not removed the curse, though they have made it bearable. What Harlan Sanders experienced is a measure of how hard life can be.

Second, life is full of obstacles. This is different from "hard." "Hard" means it can be difficult to get started in life; hard even to find a way. It was certainly that way for Harlan Sanders. But "obstacles" means once we do find a path, there will be potholes and pitfalls, troubles and snares, dangers and toils all along the way. If "hard" produces exhaustion, "obstacles" produce discouragement, even despair: "I thought this opportunity/dream/job was going to work out. And then the whole thing fell through! What's the use in even trying?" Those who pursue the path of their dreams without a realistic appraisal of obstacles run the risk of dream-ending discouragement.

Third, it's never too late. Harlan Sanders found success late in life which validates the biblical law of the harvest (see Gal. 6:7). It is built into God's economy that those who sow will reap. But it is also true we can sow errantly and on hard ground—so reaping may take time. Not only is it God's law that we reap what we sow, we will also reap more than we sow. Sow one tiny tomato seed and you will reap hundreds of seeds in a single tomato—a hundred thousand seeds on a single tomato vine. Those who overcome life's obstacles and continue to sow will reap a harvest in due time if they do not grow weary: "Let us not become weary in doing good, for at the proper time we will reap a harvest if we do not give up" (Gal. 6:9).

There are life lessons for all people in the story of Harlan Sanders. But in this chapter I want to share ten lessons for the child of God about overcoming obstacles, about not giving up, that come from the Bible's "Shepherd Psalm"—Psalm 23. David, the author, a shepherd himself, knew whereof he spoke when it came to overcoming obstacles. You recall he was anointed by God to become king of Israel at a time when King Saul was clinging to the throne, refusing to acknowledge David's right to accession. Saul hounded David all over the land of Israel trying to kill him. For several years David's path to the throne was filled with obstacles—specifically, the spears and swords of a crazed king and his soldiers.

So when David wrote the Twenty-third Psalm, "the valley of the shadow of death" was no mere poetic platitude for him. He lived in that valley for years. But he was also guided through it by the Lord his Shepherd. And that same Lord will guide us around, over, and through the obstacles we face as we journey toward our calling.

As in David's life, sometimes the seeds we sow bear fruit years after they are sown. For instance, one year my wife planted a half dozen tomato plants in different places in our yard, fully expecting some luscious fruit to grace our table that summer. Surprise! Not a single plant survived and not a single tomato was harvested.

The following summer, however, in a different place in our yard, where as far as we know no tomato had been planted, a "volunteer" tomato plant sprung up. How did a tomato seed find its way there? Had a tomato been thrown in the bushes by someone? We don't know—but we didn't complain. We just watched in amazement and enjoyed the more than two hundred tomatoes produced.

God is in charge of the harvest. Seeds get sown in different ways by different people, but God sees them all and brings them to fruition in His perfect time. Our job is to be faithful to sow and leave the harvest to God.

Lesson One: Focus on Who Is, Not What Isn't

The LORD is my shepherd, I shall not be in want.

Six months after graduating from seminary and joining the staff at my father's church, I realized I needed to find my own walking shoes. With my father's blessing I began developing plans to start a new church in San Juan Capistrano, California, just down the coast from Garden Grove, the location of the Crystal Cathedral. I approached a friend of our family who had a large tract of land on which sat numerous buildings associated with his home and business. It was a beautiful location for a new church—but not for the church I wanted to start for he had already committed the land to another ministry organization. He suggested we look for a theater or other local facility in which to meet.

So I did. Could we meet at a local theater? No. At the local shopping mall? No. At any of the numerous schools in the area? No, no and no. The last place I asked—a local community college—said yes. And that's where Capistrano Community Church met for eighteen months until that school also said no.

After revisiting all the previous facilities whose officials said no eighteen months before, and being told no again, I went back to visit with the family friend to whom I had first spoken. And due to some amazing changes since we talked earlier, the family decided to gift the property to the Crystal Cathedral. And we were given permission to use one of the buildings as a meeting place for our new church, the very place I felt we were to begin the church originally.

It took nearly two years for the Lord, my Shepherd, to test my faith and teach me to patiently wait on His provision.

Trust the Lord who is your Shepherd when your dream is blocked or delayed by obstacles.

Lesson Two: Accept God's Gift of Comfort

He makes me lie down in green pastures.

The lowest point of my life was the day I stood before the church I started to tell them my wife had filed for a divorce. We married young, during college, probably too early in retrospect, but I was confident our faith and love would be sufficient to carry us through whatever came. But it wasn't.

What was I to do then? Burdened with shame and guilt over the failure of my marriage, I felt leaving the ministry was the only option with integrity. But God had comfort for me I didn't expect. First, from my congregation who gathered to embrace me after that Sunday's service. After healing with the balm of their love the following week, I stood in the pulpit again to thank them for being God's hands of comfort in my life.

I told them about the majestic California redwood trees whose roots grow shallow and wide instead of deep. But in a redwood grove, the roots of all the trees grow together, every tree gaining support from every other tree. As a single tree, redwoods cannot stand. But as part of a group they become the tallest and strongest trees in the world.

I had to learn to receive the comfort and strength God was giving me through my church. Without them, I would have fallen from the weight of my burden.

Receive God's comfort when you encounter obstacles in your path.

Lesson Three: Be Willing to Follow

He leads me beside quiet waters, He restores my soul.

Although my sister, Carol, had a leg amputated when she was thirteen as a result of a motorcycle accident, it hasn't slowed her down one bit.

When I, a rookie snow skier from Southern California, visited her in Winter Park, Colorado, in the winter of 1984, she became my guide. After laughing at the clothes I brought from California for skiing, she took me to a local outfitter and got me dressed for success on the slopes.

Admittedly, my pride took a beating that day: a strong, athletic Southern California beach jockey being schooled by his handicapped little sister. But what I saw on the slopes later that day caused me to change my thinking.

I saw blind skiers coming down the slopes with amazing dexterity, responding to the verbal instructions of their guides who skied twenty or thirty feet ahead of them: "Slightly left, hard right, bump coming, slow down now . . ." The skiers were totally dependent on their guides and not the least bit embarrassed by their need for guidance. It was a reminder to me that everyone needs a guide at some point in life, and everyone needs *the* Guide to get through life without crashing and falling.

Stay sensitive to God's guidance through the obstacles in your path.

Lesson Four: Be Grateful for God's Cleansing

He guides me in paths of righteousness for His name's sake.

I know of nothing that can derail a life moving in the right direction faster than guilt does. That happened to a beautiful girl I'll call Laurie. Her life was normal until she turned fifteen and her father disappeared for two years. Her mother told her his absence was work related, though when he showed up again she learned he'd been in prison for embezzlement. Her parents turned on one another with Laurie caught in the middle, trying to play the role of parent to two dysfunctional adults.

When she was seventeen, her father asked her out on a date for the evening, but their destination was a gay club where she met her father's lover—something her mother knew nothing about. Not long after that, Laurie's boss invited her to dinner as a thank you for her hard work and proceeded to rape her.

Somehow, Laurie felt responsible for all her parents' problems as well as her own rape, though she had done nothing wrong. Her life was being ruined by false guilt. When she came to understand she had no reason to feel guilty, she was able to get her life back on track. Other people feel guilty because they have sinned against God and man, in which case their guilt is real!

If guilt is an obstacle in your path, ask God to forgive you and He will. That is why He extended Himself in the person of Jesus Christ, to take our sins and guilt away. It doesn't matter whether we deserve it or not; God will take it away if we ask Him.

Don't let guilt, false or real, be an obstacle that keeps you from accomplishing your purpose in life.

Lesson Five: Let God Carry You Through

Even though I walk through the valley of the shadow of death, I will fear no evil.

A year after my divorce was final, my father and I were talking together about my ministry. He said (I'm paraphrasing his words), "You have good judgment, but I have never been confident of your sincerity in dealing with people. How could you preach to brokenhearted people if your own heart had never been broken? How could you tell people to 'trust God' in the darkness when you have lived most of your life in the light? But you've changed. Since going through the darkness and death of your own marriage you have earned your credentials. You know what those to whom you are preaching feel. And you know God can do for them what He has done for you."

He was right, of course, though I didn't realize I even had that need until coming out the far end of the valley of the shadow of death. It simply stands to reason we cannot learn to let God carry us until we have fallen. But when we do, He is there to walk with us through our darkest hours.

My first semester of college wasn't the valley of the shadow of death—but it was close. Why? Because I graduated from high school without being able to read. It was more a comprehension issue than a reading issue. I could call out the words on the page but couldn't deduce the meaning of words strung together in sentences and paragraphs. Somehow I managed to graduate.

I decided to major in music in college to avoid as much reading as possible. But I had to have a foreign language to graduate, so I signed up for beginning Greek (which I knew I would need for seminary as well). I passed that semester of Greek as a gift, I think, but my professor wouldn't let me enter the second semester course without being tutored. Graciously, he volunteered to help me.

The first time we met, something seemingly miraculous happened. He listened to me read haltingly from the Greek New Testament in a way that was unintelligible to either of us. He took the text and said, "Read it like this." Listening to him read was like listening to a smooth-flowing conversation. He handed the text back to me and I began to read differently than I'd ever read before. And I wondered—*Am I supposed to read English this same way?*

I went back to my dorm room and picked up a book in English and began to read it the same way my professor told me to read Greek. It was like my eyes were opened! I actually understood what I was reading; a whole new world opened before me. God brought me through that valley in a way I've never yet fully understood.

When fear becomes an obstacle in your path, replace it with faith.

Lesson Six: Let Love Release You

For you are with me.

In December 1984 my first marrage came to an end. My wife and I were separated until our divorce was finalized; I moved into a condominium in Laguna Beach. The day after what had been the gloomiest Christmas Day of my life, I went for a walk on the beach in spite of overcast skies and mist. There was only one other person on the beach that day, a woman named Donna. We began to talk as we walked along and I told her up front, for the sake of honesty, that I was married with two children. When she seemed to wonder what a family man was doing on the beach alone on the day after Christmas, I explained that I was separated and would soon be getting the divorce papers. As it turned out, her situation was identical. She and her husband had been separated for eighteen months, headed for divorce.

We met together several times after that to talk. We swapped books and found a measure of comfort in the similarity of our circumstances and I found myself drawn to this lovely woman who made me feel better, not worse, about myself. As it turns out, Donna became my wife in due course and has become God's greatest gift of love to me.

I know God was with me that day on the beach because He introduced me to the love of my life. God's love through Donna has become the single most therapeutic part of my life.

Don't let obstacles keep you from believing you are loved.

Lesson Seven: Yield to Authority and Protection

Your rod and your staff, they comfort me.

When I was seventeen years old I announced to my parents that I was going to enter full-time ministry. They announced to me that until I was eighteen I would do as I was told—and that meant college. My freshman year in college I discovered I was impossibly underprepared to fully minister to anyone. I didn't know the Bible's original languages, didn't know the Old Testament, didn't know history or philosophy, and didn't even know how to study. So I stayed in college until I graduated, at which point I entered seminary for four more years of preparation. After that I entered the ministry under the oversight of the Reformed Church in America and the Crystal Cathedral staff.

How thankful I was God used the authoritative rod and protective staff of my parents to save me from my worthy, but woefully immature, dream of entering the ministry at age seventeen. God has no doubt put one or more "rods" and "staffs" in your life. Before you reject them, make sure it is not the hand of God holding them.

Don't mistake a signpost of authority or protection for an obstacle in your path.

Lesson Eight: Remember That God Is with You

You prepare a table before me in the presence of my enemies.

I mentioned earlier about my sister's motorcycle accident and the result-ing amputation of her leg. But it wasn't as simple as that. She was hos-pitalized for nine months, missing an entire year of school, church, sports—everything. She lost twenty-six pints of blood immediately fol-lowing the accident. Since the human body only holds twelve to thirteen pints, she was losing it as quickly as they could put it in her. When the paramedics arrived on the scene, they couldn't detect a pulse. She sur-vived, literally, by the grace of God.

For months Carol battled infections, internal injuries, and the psy-chological stress of having lost her leg. As a result of the severity of her injuries, I was nervous the first time I went to visit her once she was stable. When I entered her hospital room I found her sitting up in bed and smiling. She said, "Bob, I know God has great things in store for my life. I am going to be able to minister to people who normally wouldn't pay attention to me. God is using me for something great. He's prepar-ing me for something special." Carol was sitting at a feast-table of God's grace, and has been ever since.

Acknowledge God's presence and provision even when all you can see are obstacles in your path.

Lesson Nine: Live in God's Anointing

You anoint my head with oil; my cup overflows.

Anointing with oil was a common practice in biblical days, especially the Old Testament. It was a sign of God's blessing and favor on a person com-missioned to serve in a particular way. Jesus was anointed by the Holy Spirit when He was baptized in the Jordan River by John the Baptist.

In the same way, we who have been baptized by the Spirit into the body of Christ need to see that gift as God's anointing—a permanent anointing in which we live. The indwelling Spirit of God becomes our source of power for life and ministry. I desperately needed that anointing early in 1984. I was sure that my divorce had consigned me to a lifetime of celibacy on the fringe of ministry. But by God's anointing, He led me to a different conclusion. Through study of Scripture and counsel with others (especially a dream my father had), I gained confidence that God wanted me to love again, even to marry and build a family to His glory.

I grieve for those I meet in life whose paths have been blocked by obstacles; who need God's anointing to find their way through; who need His overflowing grace in their cup.

Seek and receive the anointing of God's Spirit to help you navigate through the obstacles in your path.

Lesson Ten: Prepare for Problems in Front of You and Goodness and Love Behind You

Surely goodness and love will follow me all the days of my life, and I will dwell in the house of the LORD forever.

One Sunday morning I interviewed a well-known Canadian business-man on the *Hour of Power* television broadcast. After he shared his testi-mony, I asked, "What happened to you after you made Christ the center of your life?"

He looked at me and said very honestly, "Actually, I was still faced with all the problems I had been facing before I was a Christian. The problems didn't go away."

Some people believe that when they accept Christ as their Savior their new Bible will come with a "Get Out of Jail Free" card tucked within its pages. They are disappointed to discover when they open their eyes after praying to receive Christ, their problems haven't disappeared. And often, they get worse! (Remember: Satan will not be pleased that you have switched sides, and he will do everything he can to make you "repent" and switch back.)

As I said at the beginning of this chapter, life is hard whether you are a follower of Christ or not. While you will never look down your path and see it entirely free of obstacles, you will never look behind you and *not* see the goodness and love of God following you all the days of your life. That's what makes this challenging life livable!

Before you give in to your obstacles, see if you aren't being followed by God's goodness and love.

My friend, I pray you will begin to see the obstacles in your path as mere stones, not boulders, put there or allowed to be there by a God who is with you as your Shepherd. He is ready to guide, comfort, direct, anoint, and follow you until you arrive where you are going. Meditating on these ten lessons will help you get there sooner rather than later.

When we learn to
make "faith" a verb, we
will be ready to begin.

Walking by Faith

We live by faith, not by sight.

—2 Corinthians 5:7

Sally Baxter had a burden. Having grown up as an emotionally and sexually abused child, she spent most of her twenties working through issues of forgiveness, redemption, understanding, and identity. Her past had not derailed her life—she had a healthy and maturing marriage, two children who were doing well, and a part-time job as a teacher's aide at her children's school.

But she still had a burden. Partly due to her temperament—she could be driven and obsessive about things—she decided to tackle and conquer her past. She read voluminously in areas dealing with the abuses she suffered and spent time with professional therapists when she got "stuck" on something she couldn't understand or manage—especially if her inner wounds were having a negative impact on her husband and children. She even audited some master's level counseling and psychology courses at a local community college.

She made good progress. She reconciled with her parents and brought closure, from her point of view, to the impact of "the sins of the fathers" on her life. She discovered patterns of behavior preceding her parents' generation that made her even more committed to not allowing history to repeat itself in her life.

Sally's burden was not for herself. She reached a point where she knew she was over the hump—that she was going to make it. She was not going to live her life chained to something from which Christ had set her free. Her burden was for untold numbers of women who might not have found that same freedom; women who were living silent lives of suffering; women who lived with clouds of shame, remorse, bitterness, and false guilt over abuses suffered as children or young girls. She believed God wanted her to take her compassion and knowledge and empathy and drive and reach out to abused women.

But where to start? She could envision, down the road, a Christ-centered counseling ministry that would serve as an educational, therapeutic, empathetic safe-harbor for women with abuse in their past and present. She could see a product-in-process, up and running, expanding and offering services she hadn't even thought of. But what she could see with her eye of faith cost money—a building, staff, salaries, overhead. From where would that money come?

Sally and her husband, Jack (who was very supportive of the idea), invited their pastor to their home for lunch to get his perspective. Pastor Thomas knew something of Sally's background, but listened intently as she shared an overview of her abuse, her own path of healing, and the vision she had for helping other women.

"Sally," the pastor began, "—and Jack, too, since I know you've walked through a lot of this with Sally—I have to say I'm impressed with the journey you've been on. And I couldn't agree more that it sounds like this burden and vision you have is not only needed, but is being energized by the Lord. I would certainly look at it that way until He shows you something different.

"Making that assumption puts this vision of yours into a whole different category. If this is something God is calling you to do, then it is no longer a 'could do' but a 'must do.' You may remember that Paul said—'Woe is me'—if he didn't fulfill his own calling from God.

"Secondly, if this is from God, then we have to assume that for what He wants done, He is willing to provide resources. Money is never a problem for God. The problem is our lacking the faith to believe He will take us from the birth to the fruition of a vision like yours. To see this happen you'll need to learn to walk by faith and not by sight. Your faith will be the bridge over which you'll walk to get from today to the vision you have in your mind's eye.

"Third, while I can't speak for the church board, I believe I can say they will have no hesitation in encouraging this vision and providing an umbrella of support under which it can be nourished. You might plan to come to a meeting in the near future to share a summary of what you'd like to accomplish.

"Finally, as you know, buildings and counselors are just means to an end. The end is women who need healing. So let's begin to pray that God will show you where to start; that He will lead you to someone who needs the ministry of love and encouragement you have to offer. That might grow into a small group—or several—or a seminar or weekend retreat. Who knows? That's what's exciting about walking by faith. God gives us the script a step at a time.

"Your job is to believe, unswervingly, that God wants women made whole in ways you haven't thought of yet; He will use you as His instrument."

WHEN MOTIVATIONAL SPEAKER BILL IRWIN talks to audiences, he often includes stories from his 1990 hike of the famous Appalachian Trail. He will sometimes include these lines which invariably bring an explosion of laughter from the audience:

"On November 21, 1990, I stopped a hundred yards short of [completing] the Appalachian Trail. I only had a hundred yards to go. And for the first time in eight and a half months, I chuckled when I thought, *If I don't do something real stupid, I'm going to make it!*"

Did you explode with laughter when you read that short paragraph? I'm betting you didn't, and I wouldn't have either if I didn't know Bill Irwin personally. The idea that he might stumble in the last hundred yards of a 2,175-mile hike only becomes "funny" when you realize that Bill Irwin is blind. That's right—completely, legally blind. He is a man who navigated deep ravines, climbed over rocky crags, crossed swollen mountain streams, and sometimes endured days on end of rain and wind chills of seventy degrees below zero, for nearly 2,200 miles from Georgia to Maine—all without the benefit of sight. That's what makes the idea of him "doing something real stupid" on the last, level hundred yards, amazingly, self-deprecatingly, hilarious.

Here's a small challenge for you: When you are finished reading this chapter, before you stand up from where you're sitting—close your eyes. As long as it's safe (say, in your own home—not on an airplane or at a busy intersection), try navigating to your next spot with your eyes closed. Even if you're somewhere very familiar, at home or your office, you'll be amazed at what a challenge it is to move without whacking your shin and cracking your head on something immovable in your path.

Now think about doing that for 2,175 miles along the Appalachian Trail. Bill Irwin was the first, and so far, the only blind person to hike the entire trail. And after you stumble from your living room to your bedroom in complete darkness, you'll understand why no one else has done it.

Bill Irwin was a recovered alcoholic when he decided to honor God's blessings in his life by doing something extraordinary; doing something that would show the world that with God all things are possible. He went blind at age twenty-eight from an eye disease and at age forty-nine decided it was time to do something totally impossible for a blind person to do—or so it would seem. He was not an experienced hiker, but chose hiking the Appalachian Trail (AT) as a way to say it is possible to walk by faith and not by sight.

Yes, he had help along the way—but not as much as you might imagine. His German shepherd seeing-eye dog, Orient, was his companion from start to finish. His son and an AT volunteer prepared audio tapes describing mile markers on the trail and their relationship to towns, post offices, hostels, AT shelters, restaurants, and other facilities. His church in Burlington, North Carolina, prepared supply packages they mailed ahead of time to post offices along the way.

For almost all of his 259 days on the trail, Bill Irwin and Orient hiked alone. He learned to read trail sign markers with his fingers, feeling the letters routed into the wooden signs. Orient learned to find the small white markers that keep hikers on the trail from start to finish, much as a seeing-eye dog learns to read traffic lights and protect their masters in the middle of a big city. And Bill learned to trust Orient's leading, and his own intuition, about the right way to go.

As you can imagine, Bill fell a lot—sometimes scores of times in a single day. He broke a rib, wore out seven pairs of hiking boots, six ski poles, and three pack frames before he finished. But he did finish, which is more than most people who start the AT can say. More than a thousand people a year start to hike the trail with only 20–25 percent finishing. Upward of 10 percent quit within a week—even with the benefit of eyesight. The idea that Bill Irwin completed the entire trail without sight is one of the most remarkable human achievements in history.

Bill Irwin has continued to walk by faith since 1990. He has hiked more than five thousand miles on trails all over the world and serves as a sought-after consultant, trainer, and counselor. He has appeared on the *Hour of Power* television program, and my father wrote the introduction to his 1992 book *Blind Courage* which details his odyssey on the Appalachian Trail. He has proven there is something more important than sight for success in this life—faith.

Walking by Faith

For those pursuing a successful journey through this life, Bill Irwin's story is a perfect example of the possibility—indeed, the necessity—of walking by faith and not by sight. When it comes to the Bible's most straightforward statement on this necessity I prefer the New American Standard Bible's translation of 2 Corinthians 5:7: "For we walk by faith, not by sight." Some translations read, "We *live* by faith . . ." which is certainly theologically correct (see Rom. 1:17). But in a book about finding our own walking shoes, I like the sense of motion that comes with the word "walk."

The Greek word Paul uses in 2 Corinthians 5:7 is *peripateo*, from which we get our word *peripatetic*, which means to walk about from place to place or to travel on foot. Bible scholars often describe the ministry of the apostle Paul as a peripatetic ministry because he walked all over Palestine, Asia Minor, and some of Europe. And that's the literal meaning of the Greek word: *peri* means "about," and *pateo* means "to tread"—therefore, to walk about.

I also find it interesting that Paul didn't say we "arrive" by faith, but that we walk, or live, by faith. While it is certainly true Christians will arrive at their eternal destination by faith, Paul's emphasis in 2 Corinthians 5 is that, until we get there, we walk by what we know, not by what we see.

His point in this passage is that we would "prefer to be away from the body and at home with the Lord" (v. 8). But until that time comes, our life in the body is a life of faith—a spiritual life, not a sensory life.

Since childhood we have been taught human beings have five senses: sight, taste, touch, smell, and hearing. And from a physical perspective, that's certainly right. But I also believe there is a sixth sense which exists as a potential in every human being—a spiritual sense by which we communicate with God. I haven't seen, tasted, touched, smelled, or heard God lately, but I have definitely communicated with Him. How? By my spirit in union with His Spirit.

This is what Paul is referring to in 1 Corinthians 2:13–14:

This is what we speak, not in words taught us by human wisdom but in words taught by the Spirit, expressing spiritual truths in spiritual words. The man without the Spirit does not accept the things that come from the Spirit of God, for they are foolishness to him, and he cannot understand them, because they are spiritually discerned.

He compares this spiritual sense to the physical senses in verses 9–10:

However, as it is written: "No eye has seen, no ear has heard, no mind has conceived what God has prepared for those who love him"—but God has revealed it to us by his Spirit. The Spirit searches all things, even the deep things of God.

There is a whole realm of truth from which human beings are cut off apart from a relationship with the Spirit of God. Conversely, as soon as our human spirit is quickened to new life—as soon as we are "born again," to use Jesus' words—we suddenly have a new set of antennae; a new way of receiving guidance and help in our life.

At that point we begin to "hear" and understand what God is saying to us. We begin to see life from His divine perspective instead of being limited by our human perspective.

I have read that the African impala, one of the most beautiful and graceful of the antelope family, can leap to a vertical height of ten feet while covering a horizontal distance of thirty feet. Yet these beautiful animals can easily be kept in an enclosure in a zoo when surrounded by a solid fence or barrier no more than three feet high. They simply will not jump if they cannot see where their feet will land. They do not know that the earth is as solid on the other side of the wall as it is on their side. As a result, their world is limited to only that which they can see.

That is an apt picture of the difference between human sight and spiritual sight. Humanly speaking we often cannot see "over the wall"—where our feet will land if we decide to step out in faith to accomplish something we believe God is calling us to do. But with spiritual discernment—with our sixth, spiritual sense—our faith can lead us to step out. We can gain confidence that though we cannot see what is on the other side of the barrier that constrains us, God can. He would never call us to go somewhere or do something that was not the right thing to do.

I have read a story set in the terrible days of the German blitzkrieg, or bombing, of London in World War II. A father and his son were in a building hit by a bomb from a German plane. Running from the burning building while holding his son's hand the father spied a huge bomb crater deeper than he was tall. He jumped into it and turned and held out his arms for his son. "Jump! I'll catch you," he yelled to his son, silhouetted against the night sky on the edge of the crater.

The terrified child looked into the black hole and screamed to his father, "But I can't see you!"

"But I can see *you!*" the father yelled back. And the boy jumped into his father's arms, not because of what he could see but because of who could see him.

That is precisely what it means to walk by faith in God, not by sight. We do not walk through this life based on our five senses alone. Indeed, we submit to what those senses may be telling us ("I can't see any way this will work!") with a spirit of faith we ask God to help—to release us from being bound by the limitations of our human senses and perceptions.

Does that mean we do away with common sense? Of course not! God gave us our five senses as receptors—as gates through which information about this world passes. The point of walking by faith is to not be limited by that information. Walking by faith is not an *irrational* lifestyle, devoid of reason. Rather, it is a *transrational* lifestyle; it goes beyond human reason. Walking by faith is a lifestyle of adding God's perspective to ours. And divine reason always trumps human reason.

Here's what it means to add God's reasoning to our own. I read about a fire in the Harlem district of New York—an apartment building was ablaze and a young blind girl was leaning out a fourth-floor window above an alleyway too narrow for a fire truck to get in and raise a ladder. Firemen were standing below the window with a net calling for the little girl to jump into the net—a net she couldn't see. Suddenly the little girl's father arrived on the scene and took the bullhorn from the firemen and explained to his daughter that he was there, the firemen were there, and they had a net to catch her safely when she jumped. Only then did that which seemed unreasonable to a blind girl in one moment—jumping out of a window into a net she couldn't see—become perfectly reasonable in the next moment. She relaxed and dropped off the window ledge into the firemen's net without injury.

What changed in that situation? Only one thing: the presence of a voice she recognized; a voice she trusted completely; the voice of her father. When she added that variable into the mix, everything changed. Unreasonable became reasonable. And death became life.

We are like that little blind girl at times. While she was literally blind, we sometimes become figuratively blind. We get stuck on the ledge of life, frozen by what we cannot see or what we do not understand. It is only when the voice of our heavenly Father is added to the mix that we have the ability to relax and know we will be safe. He is able to explain that what we cannot see is nevertheless something we should do. That is what it means to walk by faith.

Learning to Walk by Faith

If you were tasked with building a bridge across a wide gorge, where would you begin? In front of you are two things: a deep gorge and an architectural rendering of what the finished bridge is to look like. How would you get from no bridge to bridge? In a less-technical day than ours, I have heard it might be accomplished as follows:

Assuming there are people on the other side of the gorge, you could take a bow and shoot an arrow from your side of the gorge to the other. Attached to the arrow would be the thinnest of threads or string. When the arrow landed on the other side, the string would be used to pull across a slightly thicker, stronger piece of twine. Then that twine would be used to pull across a small diameter rope. Then the rope would be used to pull across a larger rope; and then the rope, a cable; then the cable, a chain, and so on. Where the two sides of the gorge were once connected by nothing, now they are connected by a chain, a link from which further progress can be made.

Walking by faith is a process of beginning where you are with what you have, taking small steps that have the potential for becoming large steps. Bill Irwin tells how, in traversing the Appalachian Trail, he might make ten miles in a ten-hour day. One mile per hour doesn't sound like much. But, he says, doing two hundred ten-mile days results in a two thousand-mile walk if you look at them as one day at a time. Faith sees the two thousand-mile journey; sight sees today's ten miles from here to there, and tomorrow's, and tomorrow's.

Learning to walk by faith is not easy. When Jesus was raised from the dead there were some of His followers who had a hard time believing it was true. And Jesus had a special commendation for those who believed without seeing: "Because you have seen me, you have believed," He said to some who were with Him. But "blessed are those who have not seen and yet have believed" (John 20:29). Believing without seeing is the essence of walking by faith and is something Jesus appreciates.

The apostle Peter acknowledged the tension between seeing and believing when he wrote, "Though you have not seen [Christ], you love him; and even though you do not see him now, you believe in him and are filled with an inexpressible and glorious joy" (1 Pet. 1:8).

That should be true of every single person who is a follower of Christ. We believe in someone we have never seen and anticipate spending eternity with Him. The world says, "I'll believe it when I see it!" Christians say, "I'll see it when I believe it!"

Have you heard the story about the man who was crossing the desert and ran out of water? He was about to die of thirst when he came upon an abandoned shack at the base of a cliff. And sticking out of the ground was a pipe with a pump handle attached to it. Sitting next to the pipe was a sealed jug filled with water and a note: "This well has never run dry, but the pump must be primed. Pour the jug of water into the top of the pump and then begin pumping the handle. After you have drunk your fill, replace the water in the jug for the next person to use."

What would you have done? If you drank the water in the jug you would get no more. But if you poured the water into the pump and it didn't work, you might die. This is a case of "believing, then seeing"—it takes an act of faith before receiving that which will change or save your life.

Just like a toddler learns to walk physically, so a Christian must learn to walk by faith. Let's draw some analogies from Bill Irwin's two thousand two hundred miles on the Appalachian Trail to see what might help us take those faith-steps with increasing confidence.

1. Ask for Directions

When Bill Irwin would lose his way on the trail, or get disoriented or turned around, he would stop and sit down. For him, the quickest way to injury or possible death was wandering off into dangers he couldn't see. So he would literally stop, take out his emergency whistle, and blow it every few minutes. Usually, within a few hours or half a day, another hiker would come along and hear his whistle and direct him and Orient back onto the trail.

We often hear it said that staying in motion is critical to success; that it's easier for God to guide us if we're moving. That's true unless we know we're moving in the wrong direction. It takes time to develop spiritual discernment. If you don't have it in a particular place in your journey, STOP! Don't wander into foolish or dangerous ground because you're too embarrassed to say, "I'm lost. Please help me."

2. Create a Support Group

Bill's church in North Carolina was his primary support group. I've already mentioned how they mailed support packages to post offices along the trail. They were there for him at the beginning and were there for him at the end. A group of twenty church members drove a small bus from North Carolina to Maine to celebrate the completion of his quest.

Their presence was, I'm sure, a key reason he didn't want to do anything "really stupid" in that last hundred yards.

How many people does it take to bring a baby into the world today? While it might be only two or three for a home birth, it takes six to twelve in a hospital between the OB/GYN, a pediatrician or neonatologist, and a bevy of nurses and support staff. If you can birth a vision for your life and bring it to maturity by yourself, more power to you. But I would encourage you not to try. Many a vision has been still-born because there was no one there to spank life into it when first it appeared!

Gather some people around you who will encourage you and believe in you *and who will not laugh at your dream!* Proverbs 15:22 says, "Plans fail for lack of counsel, but with many advisers they succeed." And this is true in two ways, at least one of which applies to you today.

First, you may have a vision related to a calling or purpose in your life—something you believe God wants you to do. A support group will help that dream become a reality.

Second (and this applies to every one of us), your very life is a vision. You may not have a specific, detailed "thing" God wants you to accomplish right now (begin a new adventure, start a ministry, create your own business, go on the mission field). That's fine. But that doesn't mean your life doesn't have purpose. It only means God wants your purpose to be to pursue Him with your whole heart while He expands or refines or develops something further for you to do. And you need a support group around you for that. Are you in a small group that meets for prayer, fellowship, and accountability? If not, I encourage you to find one, or begin one, or develop some similar type of support network around your life. It is too easy to wander off the trail without it. If you want some assistance, go to crystalcathedral.org/housesofpower.

3. Find a "Friend"

While I've focused on Bill Irwin's amazing accomplishment of walking the Appalachian Trail by faith, let's be realistic: it's not likely he could have accomplished that heroic feat without his guide-dog, Orient. For 259 days, Orient was, in biblical terms, a friend that stuck closer than a brother (see Prov. 18:24).

In the Old Testament, the word "friend" often occurred in a covenant context. The chief example is when Abraham, with whom God made a covenant, is called the friend of God (see 2 Chron. 20:7; Isa. 41:8; James 2:23). Jesus called those with whom He was forging a new covenant, "friends" (see John 15:15). When Proverbs 18:24 says there is a friend who sticks closer than a brother, it's referring to a friend whose love and faithfulness are thicker than blood; a friend who values your life as more important than his own (John 15:13); a friend with whom you have forged a covenant-like bond—like the bond between Jonathan and David (see 1 Sam. 18:3–4; 20:16–17).

This kind of friend is one who will say what Jonathan said to David: "Whatever you want me to do, I'll do for you" (1 Sam. 20:4). This is the same thing Jesus said to His twelve "friends:" "Ask whatever you wish, and it will be given you" (John 15:7).

Do you have a friend like that? Jesus had a support group of twelve, within which was a core group of three (Peter, James, and John), and then He had one disciple whom He seemed to have a special friendship: John, "the disciple whom Jesus loved" (John 13:23; 21:7, 20), the same disciple to whom Jesus later revealed His apocalyptic vision of the future—the book of Revelation.

If you don't have that one person to whom you can tell the secrets of your vision, ask God to bring him or her to you. If your faith weakens, your friend's faith will be there to keep you strong.

4. Get Oriented

In order to make sure he started in the right direction every morning, Bill would pitch his tent with the point headed north—that is, toward Maine as far as the Appalachian Trail was concerned. When he awoke in the morning he could move around camp without fear of getting turned around. His tent was his compass until he struck it and packed it and set off for the day.

It's easy, when talking about walking by faith, to gradually put faith in faith. That's not what we're talking about. The Christian lifestyle of walking by faith means faith in the Lord Jesus Christ, faith in the promises of God found in the Bible, and faith in the Holy Spirit to be your counselor, guide, and teacher. Faith is only as good as the object toward which faith is directed. Faith can be fuzzy or faith can be factual, rooted in time and space. That latter kind of faith is what the Bible talks about when it says we walk by faith, not by sight.

If you are not using the Bible, and a relationship with Christ, to keep you oriented on a daily basis, then your chances of wandering off the path of your journey toward God's best for your life are greatly increased. Use a prayer guide, a daily Bible reading guide, a book of devotionals— something that will keep God and His truth fresh in your mind as you walk. With all the devotional resources available today there is no reason for a follower of Jesus to lose his or her spiritual way. You can sign up to receive a devotional e-mail every day at crystalcathedral.org/subscribe.

5. Get Used to Falling

I've already mentioned that Bill Irwin would fall dozens of times a day on the Appalachian Trail. He expected it and took it in stride. Babies fall hundreds of times when learning to walk. And if you are learning to walk by faith, you will fall as well. It's a given.

If you are easily discouraged by falls you will never hone your spiritual sense of discernment—that sixth sense I've talked about. When Bill would fall he would stop and listen—listen for Orient's sounds and movements; listen to the wind; listen for nearby water. He would stop, gather himself, and learn what he could about what just happened. And then he would move on until he fell again.

Those walking by faith have to learn that falling is not failing as long as you get up and continue.

Hebrews 11:6 says walking without faith is not an option for those seeking to please God and find and fulfill His purpose for their life: "But without faith it is impossible to please Him, for he who comes to God must believe that He is, and that He is a rewarder of those who diligently seek Him" (NKJV). I hope you are one of those people—one who is walking on your journey by faith. If you are, great will be your reward.

There is no limit to where
you can go when you
walk in your own shoes—
your own unique identity;
a challenge to the reader
to embrace God's design for
his or her life and begin
walking in the reality that
is his or hers alone.

Walking in Your Own Shoes

Oh yes, you shaped me first inside, then out;
you formed me in my mother's womb.
I thank you, High God—you're breathtaking!
Body and soul, I am marvelously made!
I worship in adoration—what a creation!
You know me inside and out,
you know every bone in my body;
You know exactly how I was made, bit by bit,
how I was sculpted from nothing into something.
Like an open book, you watched me grow from conception to birth;
all the stages of my life were spread out before you,
The days of my life all prepared
before I'd even lived one day.

—Psalm 139:13–16 The Message

Richard and Jan Mobley had paid their dues. He was an attorney in a large firm for twenty-five years and she an English professor at a large university for the same length of time. They were good citizens, were faithful church members, lived modest lifestyles, and had saved their money. They raised three children and put them through college, who were now finding niches in which to begin their vocational lives.

In the occasional moments when Richard and Jan had time to talk, they found themselves gradually thinking and feeling the same way about their lives: what they had been doing the last twenty-five years no longer seemed to fit whom they had become. They were satisfied with their careers in law and teaching—they worked hard and made contributions they were proud of. But they were different people now. They enjoyed a measure of success but were now thinking more about significance—a different kind of success. Not necessarily better—just different. Success that would fit them as comfortably as the jeans, sweaters, and sandals they seemed to live in at home.

They were more attentive to their own health in recent years. It became an avocation of sorts. They bought a juicing machine and began to buy as much organically grown food as they could. Without really planning to, over time they became vegetarians. They learned to fit exercise into their lives, lost weight, and were feeling better than they had in years. What they realized about their own lives now concerned them about the lives of their friends, co-workers—indeed, society in general: if we don't have physical and spiritual health, all the other success in the world won't mean much.

So what to do with these newfound priorities and concerns? Lingering over the supper table one Friday night, they began to talk in earnest—to brainstorm; to play "What if?"

"Well, here's what I would do if I could write a script for us," Richard said. "Eighteen months from now we would be the proprietors of something . . . I'm not sure what . . . a bed and breakfast? A retreat-type place? I don't know what it would be. But it would be in the mountains, not here in the city. It would be on maybe ten acres of property . . . a place where people could come and learn about a healthy lifestyle. They'd stay with us, maybe one or two couples at a time, or maybe stay in a guest cottage on the property. We'd teach them what we've learned about regaining health . . . slowing down . . . focusing on new priorities, better practices. We'd share meals together, have casual, informal classes, lots of free time for connecting with nature or taking naps or whatever. We'd have a big organic garden so people could connect with food and see how God intended it to be grown. There'd be lots of rocking chairs and porch space . . . overhead fans . . . high ceilings . . . a log home . . . Have I said enough?" he concluded, smiling at his wife's open-mouthed stare.

"Wow," Jan said, "you have been doing some thinking."

"Well, what do you think?"

Jan was quiet for a few moments before she spoke. "Well, look at us. It's Friday night and we're at home in our jeans and Birkenstocks instead of out partying in the city. It seems like we are, or at least have become, the kind of people who would do something like you just described. How did that happen? We haven't always been like this."

"I don't know. We just evolved, I guess. Or maybe matured is a better word. Maybe it's time for us to move into the next stage of our lives. I don't think either of us has any regrets about what we've done so far. But I think our best work in law and education is complete. To do more would just be repetition. It seems we've learned new things about how we want to live our lives, and maybe we ought to figure out how to share that with others."

"Well," Jan said softly, "I have to admit I agree. Let's start praying about it. But why don't we think in terms of twelve months instead of eighteen," she said smiling.

"I like it," Richard said, rising from his chair. "Before you get up, let me grab a couple of magazines on log home designs I picked up today at lunch. I was amazed at the possibilities."

WHEN I WAS PREPARING TO succeed my father as senior pastor of the Crystal Cathedral, on more than one occasion someone said to me, "You've got some mighty big shoes to fill, Robert." *The truth is I could never fit in my father's shoes*: he wears a size 10½ and I wear a size 12.

I knew what they meant, of course. But I also knew I would never be able to fill my father's shoes spiritually or figuratively any more than I could fit them physically. And thankfully, my father is wise enough and gracious enough he never expected me to fill his shoes. He knows I am a different person than he. Over time, I have no doubt the Crystal Cathedral will become a different place. I won't try to make it different, and I didn't become the pastor of the church to institute changes. I just know that as the church became what it is today under my father's oversight, it will likely change slowly over the years under mine.

And that is not wrong. I see that as reflective of the marvelous grace of God in our lives and in His plans. Just as He sets up kings and takes down kings, I believe God sets up pastors and leaders and individuals to accomplish His purposes in their lifetimes. There is no better testament to that fact than the one-sentence summary of King David's life given by the apostle Paul in Acts 13:36: "For when David had served God's purpose in his own generation, he fell asleep."

What a marvelous epitaph. There could be no higher commendation for any person than to say he or she served God's purpose in his own generation. It is one thing for history to make that evaluation of someone, but far better for each of us to be able to make that assessment of our own lives before we die.

Jesus Christ, in the beautiful prayer He prayed the night of His betrayal and arrest, said to His Father, "I have brought you glory on earth by completing the work you gave me to do" (John 17:4). That was His goal at the beginning of His earthly ministry. He told His disciples, "My food . . . is to do the will of him who sent me and to finish his work" (John 4:34). It should have come as no surprise then, to those standing around the cross when He died, to hear Him say, "It is finished" (John 19:30).

My burden in writing this book has been to encourage you to believe God has work for you to do for Him. Paul says as much in Ephesians 2:10: "For we are God's workmanship, created in Christ Jesus to do good works, which God prepared in advance for us to do." I believe David's words, quoted at the beginning of this chapter, are a glorious tribute to the care and detail God exercised when He created you and me. You and I were not created to fill anybody's shoes. God has shoes for you and me to wear that are one-off models. God made them and threw away the mold.

Yes, we are like our parents and others who influenced us in many ways. People tell me I am my father's son when it comes to preaching and ministry—and I take that as a compliment. And I am also my mother's son—but I am not either of them. I am a unique creation of God designed and destined to do things for God no one else can do. And so are you.

The spiritual shoes God made for you to walk in are just as unique as your own two feet. In our high-tech world it is possible to order shoes just the way you want them. Nike, the eight hundred-pound gorilla of sport shoes, has a Web site where you can design and accessorize a pair of running shoes just the way you want them. A whole rainbow of colors is available—the shoes change on-screen instantly as you try different color combinations. You can even have your name or other word monogrammed onto the tongue. Once you're finished, you submit the order and the shoes are produced and shipped exactly as you designed them. No one else in the world will have walking shoes like yours.

That may be a cool way to get a new pair of kicks, but it's not the best analogy for how we find our walking shoes for our journey through life. In the case of the Nike Web site we're in charge. The Web site is totally passive, responding to whatever we tell it. And it doesn't address fit at all—it's all about external appearance.

In the case of our spiritual walking shoes, that's not how it works. God is not passive. He is not a vending machine delivering an external life based on appearances only. He is a personal God much more concerned about how our life "fits" us individually. Indeed, the Bible says, as we've seen from several verses, God is the One who creates us and a purpose to match. The desires of our hearts, when we live intimately with Him, turn out to be the very purposes and dreams He designed for us (see Ps. 37:4–5; Prov. 3:5–6).

Here's a better analogy of how we get our walking shoe (I'm moving toward the best analogy I know of): In 1995 a company called Digitoe created a process for creating an exact wooden model (called a "last") of a customer's foot, around which a leather shoe is built. Video cameras capture images of the foot which are digitized on a computer in a 3-D image. That image is sent to a computer-controlled milling machine that carves a model of your foot out of a block of wood. Other computer-controlled machines cut the pieces of leather that will fit that model exactly. And voilà!—you have a pair of shoes that fit your foot exactly. (Today the same process is accomplished by lasers that take 200,000 measurements of your foot, making the fit even more exact.)

That's getting closer. With this system, you get to pick the style of shoe plus you get one that fits you perfectly. But there's still too much "computer" in the process to make it a good analogy for how God works in our lives.

The best analogy I know of for how we get our walking shoes is the centuries-old bespoke (custom-made) system still practiced among the finest craftsmen in England (and in other places as well). Take the firm of James Taylor & Son, "Bespoke Shoemakers since 1857," on Paddington Street in London. James Taylor began making fine shoes for London's best-dressed citizens, and soon his shoes were being ordered by much of the royalty of Europe. The present manager of the shop is the fifth generation of Taylor's family to hand-make shoes for a discerning clientele.

Taylor's shoemakers will travel anywhere in the world to take measurements of a customer's feet. There are measurements, consultations, fittings, adjustments—whatever is needed to make sure the shoes delivered can be worn for decades. But the process doesn't come cheap. The first pair of shoes, because of the need to construct a custom last (model), will cost you £1,350 plus Value Added Tax. At today's exchange rate, that represents a cost of $2,646.00. Since the last is paid for with your first pair, the second pair will be £200 cheaper—"only" $2,254.00.

Trust me—I'm not quoting these figures from memory. These aren't the kind of shoes I buy. But I like the concept: a real-live person measuring, consulting, talking, discerning, fitting, adjusting—all with the goal of creating walking shoes for me in which no one else in the world would be comfortable. I think that's how God creates spiritual walking shoes for me and for you.

And I also like the price. The James Taylor & Son shoes don't come cheap. But neither do the walking shoes from the Father, Son & Spirit.

God paid an infinitely expensive price—the life of His own Son—to make it possible for us to enter a personal relationship with Him and get "fitted" for a life of purpose and meaning. He patiently lets us try out our life and see how it fits. He allows us time to work our way through the ups and downs of life until we begin to get comfortable with what He designed for us. And at some point we say, "Lord, I think this fits! I like these walking shoes You have created for me. I believe I can walk this way, stay on this path, for the rest of my life. Thank You that You'll be there all the time to make sure the fit stays perfect. And thank You for paying for these walking shoes out of Your own resources. Thank You for giving me something I could never afford to give myself—a life that fits me perfectly."

Getting Fitted for Your Walking Shoes

In the previous chapters I approached the theme of this book fourteen different ways: You are unique and valuable. Created by God in His image, you were designed to represent Him on planet Earth and do His good works. But you were also created to be wonderfully fulfilled in the process—so satisfied you would never look anywhere beyond God's kingdom for fulfillment in this life. To experience that satisfaction and fulfillment in life we have to get reconnected with God. That's why Christ came and died—to remove the barriers of sin and self-centeredness that have kept us dissatisfied with life.

Then we have to pursue God—begin a Father-child relationship with Him so He can talk to us about our lives: who we are, what we were created to do, and how we can move toward that for His glory and our good. In the process, we learn from God that He has no other child like us; our goal is not to imitate anyone or do what someone else thinks we should do, but to find our own unique path. We were not created to fill anyone else's shoes. We were created to receive our own walking shoes from God—shoes that fit perfectly, made just for us.

I want to review the fourteen chapters that came before this one and probe a bit. I want you to think about these questions as if a custom shoemaker was fitting you for a pair of bespoke shoes. Think about them as questions to help you get fitted for your spiritual walking shoes.

Chapter 1: Designed *for* the Journey

Big Idea: God has created you as a unique individual with the potential and resources to fulfill the desires of your heart.

Do you believe that—honestly?

How do you feel about the person you see in the mirror each morning?

From where did those perceptions and opinions come?

How far are you from seeing yourself as God sees you?

To what degree are you living the life right now you believe God created you to live?

How would you answer this question if God asked you personally: "What dreams do you have for your life yet to be fulfilled?"

Chapter 2: Designed by the Journey

Big Idea: The life you have lived so far has been preparatory for the life God wants you to live.

How do you feel about your life so far? Happy/sad? Satisfied/dissatisfied?

What connections can you see between your life so far and what you believe God wants you to do in the future?

What have been the most valuable aspects of your life? What have you learned?

To what extent do you believe God has been involved in your life so far?

To what extent have you pursued His explanation about the connections between your past and future?

Chapter 3: Your Shoes Were Made for Walking

Big Idea: You are not an evolutionary accident but were created by God for a purpose.

What spiritual-emotional sense do you have of God creating you for a purpose?

Do you think God created you for a general purpose or a specific one? Why?

What do you believe is your purpose in life?

What difference does knowing one's purpose make in how he or she lives?

What correlation do you see in your life between your knowledge of your purpose and your happiness or satisfaction?

Chapter 4: All Roads Lead to Home

Big Idea: All human purposes in life are subsumed under God's ultimate purpose for His children: that they be conformed to the image of His Son, Jesus Christ.

In what way(s) would you say God's ultimate purpose is being fulfilled in your life?

How do you see the purpose of your life on earth merging with, or cooperating with, God's ultimate purpose for you?

In what ways are any pursuits in your life conflicting with God's ultimate purpose for you?

What are you doing spiritually in your life to cooperate with God's purpose to transform you into the image of Christ?

Chapter 5: Keep Your Eye on the Goal

Big Idea: The twists and turns in the path of life are best managed when viewed against the backdrop of God's purpose.

How do you react to life's "surprises"?

How patient are you at waiting to see how the "pieces" fit into the "puzzle"?

What experience(s) have you had in moving impulsively instead of waiting on God?

What experience(s) have you had in waiting on God—where resisting the impulse to "fix" something resulted in seeing God's purpose?

What lessons do you think God might want you to learn by allowing "surprises" in your life?

Chapter 6: The Journey Is the Destination

Big Idea: Because we are immortal beings on an eternal journey, the journey becomes the destination.

If you are a Christian, what does it mean to you to have been chosen by God?

How committed are you to all the parts of the journey—the "good" as well as the "bad"?

How does knowing you have been chosen for an eternal journey change your perspective on the challenging parts of the journey?

What percent of your life is lived as if you really believe you are on a journey with God as your leader?

In your life, what would change if you focused on the journey as your destination? What are the implications?

Chapter 7: When the Wrong Way Is the Right Way

Big Idea: God uses all the events of our journey to shape our identities, even the "wrong turns" we thought were failures or mistakes.

What has God shown you about your life you didn't know five, ten, or twenty years ago?

What did you have to go through to gain those insights?

What do you know now that you believe is going to shape your journey for years to come?

How should a Christian on a journey with God react when he or she experiences failure or mistakes?

Which is more important—assessing blame or looking for the insights and new directions that can come from wrong turns in life?

Chapter 8: A Divine GPS

Big Idea: God travels our journey with us to keep us on course and provide all we need.

Do you welcome God's all-seeing eye in your life—or cringe at the thought?

What effect(s) should God's continual presence in your life have on you?

To what degree do you take advantage of God's nearness to you? To what degree do you call on Him when in need like you would a best friend?

If you became committed to the idea of God's continual presence in your life, how might such a commitment add to your success on your journey?

What contradiction is there in not incorporating God into your life and then complaining about the quality of your life?

Chapter 9: Signs along the Way

Big Idea: Hearing God's voice as we travel is a critical aspect of our life-journey.

How meaningful is your prayer life to you? How meaningful do you think it is to God?

How do you spend your prayer time? Talking? Listening? Meditating on Scripture? Which would you do well to do more of?

When you pray, do you sound more like a religious person or a child talking to his or her daddy?

What have you asked God for that, in hindsight, you're glad He didn't give you?

How well do you think you hear God's "voice"? How could you hear it more clearly?

Chapter 10: Motion Is Not the Same as Progress

Big Idea: In order to grow up before we grow old, we need to choose wisely that which we embrace on our journey.

Would you say there is more motion or more progress in your life?

What parts of your life would you label "progress" in the last year? In the last five years?

What are you trying to make progress toward? What are your goals?

Why do you think there hasn't been more progress?

To what degree is your life reflective of our motion-oriented culture? Whose fault is that? How might that change?

Chapter 11: Setting Your Direction

Big Idea: It's important to decide on a definition for success: God's or the world's.

How successful would you say you have been in your life? By what (or whose) standard are you judging?

How open are you to mid-course corrections in life—finding and profiting from something you weren't expecting? That is, do you resist change or embrace it?

To what extent do you think God is in the ideas and dreams you have?

What difference would it make to you if you believed God was behind, perhaps even the originator of, your ideas and dreams?

How happy do you think God gets when He sees you happy and fulfilled? What is the source of your answer to that question?

Chapter 12: Be Prepared

Big Idea: Few people complete journeys who fail to make adequate preparations.

Which preparations are more important for life's journey—material/ tangible preparations or spiritual/emotional ones?

At which kind of preparation have you done better in your life?

How would you correlate your success in life with the kinds of preparations you've made?

How parallel are your thoughts with God's thoughts about life? What efforts do you make to bring yours closer to His?

If being born again by faith in Christ is the only way to get God's perspective, how prepared are you? How do you know you are born again?

Chapter 13: Potholes and Pitfalls

Big Idea: Few people complete journeys who fail to negotiate and overcome obstacles.

What have been the biggest obstacles you've faced in life? How well do you think you've overcome them?

What obstacles do you see standing in the way of your dreams at present? What would you have to do to remove them?

How does pleasing God figure into your strategies for removing obstacles in your life? Do your strategies include anything to which God would say no?

How "coachable" are you? Is it more important to do things your way or to implement advice that would help you remove obstacles?

How has being a Christian impacted your view of obstacles in your path to success?

Chapter 14: Walking by Faith

Big Idea: Walking by faith is the only way to travel on a journey with God.

How much of your life is based on faith and how much on sight? That is, how trusting of God are you?

When was the last time you stepped out and did something by faith, the results of which you couldn't see beforehand?

What scares you the most about walking by faith?

Why is it inconsistent to trust God for eternity but not for tomorrow?

What would you be doing five years from now if resources weren't an issue?

Getting Fit for the Journey

On October 31, 1983, Korean Airlines flight 007 left Anchorage, Alaska, on a direct flight to Seoul, Korea. But it was never to arrive. Within a matter of hours the plane was intercepted by Soviet fighter jets and shot out of the sky. There were no survivors.

There was international outrage over the incident, of course. Why would Soviet fighters shoot down an unarmed civilian airliner? The official answer was that the Korean Airlines flight violated Soviet airspace. Apparently, no communication was established between Soviet authorities and the misguided plane. Being unaware of the plane's intent (was it friend or foe?), the decision was made to shoot it down.

Whether the Soviets made the right decision is left to history to decide. What is important for us is to understand how the airliner got so far off course. How did a plane headed for Korea end up over the former Soviet Union?

It was ultimately discovered that, unbeknownst to the plane's crew, the computer running the flight navigation system contained a one-and-one-half degree routing error. Immediately after takeoff—indeed, for the first hundred or so miles—the error was undetectable. But the further the plane flew, the larger the gap between the right path and the wrong path became. Several hundred miles out, the gap was large enough to take the plane into Soviet airspace instead of flying along the coast of that country.

Matters which are virtually undetectable at the outset can have serious ramifications in due course. When it comes to our life-journey, a small failure to prepare, a tiny chink in our moral armor, a loose thread in the fabric of our faith, an ignored piece of advice, a minor error in plotting our future course—those factors and others can mean the difference between success and failure down the road.

To keep that from happening we need to keep our ears tuned continually to the voice and promptings of the Holy Spirit. He is our counselor and our guide. He is the One who puts a check in our spirit or a hesitancy in our step—for good reasons. Yet it is amazingly easy, given the decibel level of our lives, to miss His leading. Or, if we do sense it, to shrug it off as the effects of the bad pizza we had for lunch. We desperately need the help of the One who can see past, present, and future at the same time, and who knows us better than we know ourselves.

To that end, I encourage you to draw near to God on a daily basis. Have your quiet time or devotional/prayer time faithfully. Meditate upon God's Word so you can learn to think His thoughts (see Ps. 1). Live your life in a moment-to-moment, conversational way with the Lord. Talk to Him as you travel your path. Ask Him for guidance and protection. Thank the Holy Spirit for every little thing He does that keeps you moving forward.

Don't put limits on yourself or on God. Dream big! Consider what God has done in the universe and imagine what His power and presence in your life might accomplish. Paint pictures—literal and figurative (make a dream poster plastered with pictures of what you want to accomplish)—of your dream. Talk to yourself, to God, and to your trusted friends about your dreams.

Start with achievable and measurable goals. Don't be afraid to fall. Develop confidence—first in God and then in God-in-you. Become a positive person and make friends with positive people. Be open to change and mid-course corrections. Don't give up. Hold on to hope. Develop an attitude of gratitude. Help others achieve their dreams. When you go to bed at night thank God for His mercy, His grace, and His blessings in your life. And remind Him you are trusting Him to help you discover and fulfill His purpose for your life.

If your path and my path cross one day, I look forward to hearing that you are pursuing your purpose and fulfilling your dream. And looking down, I expect to see you wearing your walking shoes.

ABOUT THE AUTHOR

ROBERT A. SCHULLER succeeded his father, Dr. Robert H. Schuller, as the second senior pastor of the Crystal Cathedral Ministries and its internationally televised *Hour of Power* program. Schuller has written twelve books, including the best-seller *Dump Your Hang-Ups Without Dumping Them on Others*. His most recent book, coauthored with Dr. Douglas DiSiena, is entitled *Possibility Living—Add Years to Your Life and Life to Your Years with God's Health Plan*. Schuller has four children and resides in Laguna Beach, California, with his wife, Donna. You can learn more about Schuller and his ministries at www.crystalcathedral.org and www.hourofpower.org.